Date: 6/4/21

176.4 MCG
McGuire, Laura,
Creating cultures of consent :
a guide for parents and

Creating Cultures
of Consent

Creating Cultures of Consent

A Guide for Parents and Educators

Laura McGuire

ROWMAN & LITTLEFIELD
Lanham • Boulder • New York • London

Published by Rowman & Littlefield
An imprint of The Rowman & Littlefield Publishing Group, Inc.
4501 Forbes Boulevard, Suite 200, Lanham, Maryland 20706
www.rowman.com

6 Tinworth Street, London, SE11 5AL, United Kingdom

British Library Cataloguing in Publication Information Available

Library of Congress Cataloging-in-Publication Data

Names: McGuire, Laura, 1987– author.
Title: Creating cultures of consent : a guide for parents and educators /
    Laura McGuire.
Description: Lanham : Rowman & Littlefield, [2021] | Includes bibliographical
    references. | Summary: "A blended conversation for bringing consent
    education to the classroom and home"— Provided by publisher.
Identifiers: LCCN 2020046483 (print) | LCCN 2020046484 (ebook) |
    ISBN 9781475850963 (cloth) | ISBN 9781475850970 (epub)
Subjects: LCSH: Sexual consent—United States. | Teenagers—
    Sexual Behavior—United States. | Sex instruction—United States. | Rape—
    United States—Prevention.
Classification: LCC HQ32 .M388 2021 (print) | LCC HQ32 (ebook) | DDC
    176/.4—dc23
LC record available at https://lccn.loc.gov/2020046483
LC ebook record available at https://lccn.loc.gov/2020046484

∞™ The paper used in this publication meets the minimum requirements of
American National Standard for Information Sciences—Permanence of Paper for
Printed Library Materials, ANSI/NISO Z39.48-1992.

This book is dedicated to my children, Emmanuel and Lily-Marie. May you and all of your descendants be agents in the creation of consent culture. I pray that consent becomes a paradigm in which you view the world and a gift you give to everyone you interact with.

Contents

Preface

I often say my students are my greatest teachers. There are always things I haven't ever considered or understood the impact of until one of them brings it up; something I strongly encourage them to do.

Through this process, I have been reminded that sometimes the first "sex education" a child receives comes in the form of being abused or raped. That being undocumented means that accessing health care and police protection is not often a viable or realistic option. That not everyone has the homelife, family, or resources to feel safe and loved in the ways that other children do. Because of this we must be mindful to create education that thinks first of those most in need and whose messages are tailored to every child and teen's reality.

I have been humbled by the violence my LGBTQ young people face at home daily, when we live in a time that pretends that this fight is over. By having diverse teachers and outlets for student input and participation, we begin to open the doors of fellowship and understanding, and these conversations start to become what they are meant to be: inclusive and approachable.

Everything I am about to say in this book is based on my personal lens and my innately limited worldview. Every person I have interviewed here is speaking from their own unique experience. We are all products of our culture, created not in a vacuum but in a myriad of social constructs, reactions, and interpretations.

No matter what research says or how many first-person narratives I gather, I am limited; all authors and experts are finite, in what we know and what we access. This is why decolonizing and looking at consent through many eyes, ears, and voices are vital to moving this discussion to the next plain.

Despite these innate limitations, I passionately put forward this book to you, dear readers. I wrote the book I wish I had when I started my work and began my family. A book that not only gives clear direction to the topic at hand but provides a holistic approach to addressing prevention, response, and healing from a research-informed perspective.

I write this book from a multifaceted lens: mother, teacher, scholar, and survivor. I live my messages in my homelife, profession, and spiritual work. Creating a culture of consent began with creating the world I needed as a child, caught up in the web of victim-blaming and shame that comes from a Catholic and Baptist upbringing. The messages I received about my body, my right to enforce physical and emotional boundaries, and my right to experience pleasurable and purposeful relationships were far from desirable. As much work as has been done, these narratives are still playing out with youth today—oftentimes because their parents are unsure of what the alternative would be.

I write this book for all my fellow survivors. Survivors of stalking, harassment, child abuse, sexual trauma, and domestic violence. Being a mom, and a mother of fellow survivors, creates an additional layer of both imperative and dismay. Trying to heal and grow the next generation means facing the deepest recesses of our pain, which is why so many choose to avoid it all together. Unless we face our trauma, we cannot break the bonds of intergenerational suffering or work to create new norms and scripts for ourselves and our families.

As teachers we are often some of the loudest voices in a child's life. We spend day after day, year after year, with minds that are developing at a faster rate than they ever will again. In homes where adult trauma is not being healed and addressed, we can be the one adult who becomes the beacon of light for children seeking an alternative for the stories they see played out at home. Teaching for me is a sacred calling and contract. Any student that I have I am there to teach and be of service to for life. It is a holy and humbling calling to impart wisdom and knowledge to the next generation—and what better a lesson to focus on than creating a world where consent is centralized and normalized.

I have had the incredible honor of teaching fellow teachers, counselors, and administrators what I have learned from my years in the classroom and as a program developer in higher education in the government. My work in ending sexual violence, working with survivors, and helping offenders come to terms with what they have done has taught me more things than one workshop can ever contain. One of my goals in writing this book is to lay down the foundational pieces that have formulated the cornerstones for my work so that when I consult or train further on these topics, my audience is coming prepared to go to the next level with our discussions.

It is with great love that I now offer this book up to you to take and learn from. I know that there are still so many conversations yet to have that are not covered here and so I hope that you choose to engage and reach out to me afterward. Remember that in all great ventures we start with a single step, and picking up this book and reading it means you are well on your way to being an agent of change and a messenger of consent culture.

Introduction

In the era post #MeToo consent conversations seem to be popping up everywhere. Now that the mainstream media has caught on to the topic, or the use of the buzzword, "consent," it may lead to many thinking that the concept of affirmative consent must have materialized out of thin air. For those of us who have worked tirelessly to bring these paradigms and calls-to-action to light for decades we are both grateful for the recent exposure and at the same time frustrated to see our previous efforts often swept under the rug.

I have witnessed a complex and multifaceted concept, such as consent, be watered down and misused, even weaponized, in certain spaces. This leads to people feeling offended or repulsed by something that should be approachable and applicable to everyone. Part of these negative reactions stems from feeling excluded in these discussions. It is my intention to open up the silos that have kept many from feeling like consent was a conversation they could be a part of—something that can be applied to anyone's life.

Consent, as a moral imperative, is nothing new to the human experience or education. It is, however, new to many born to a world forever transgressed by colonization and gender inequality. As someone who has studied the trauma enacted by these frameworks, I find great hope and joy in the knowledge that in many parts of the world cultures have existed without rape or domestic violence for generations and even more are moving in the direction now, creating new culture norms and healing the wounds of those before.

For all that we discuss in the beginning of the book about the problem and its magnitude let us not think that the issue is the story. Instead let each chapter guide you on a path of hope and solutions. Too often we come to conversations with a list of complaints and grievances but no actionable tools to making things better. This book is one tool in that toolbox: one that offers conversation starters to have with youth, ideas for community organizing, and seeds to be planted on not only how to enact change but how to build lasting and inclusive changes.

In focusing on the solution, we put our sights on what we want to create: a world where everyone feels safe, heard, and loved; where survivors are believed; where justice is restorative; and where someone not valuing affirmative consent in all interpersonal interactions is seen as the exception not the rule.

The first step is always the hardest. From where do we even begin? Sexual violence seems so pervasive. We see stories of peers, family members, faith leaders, and medical providers all ignoring children's human rights to safety and bodily autonomy. Spaces and titles that were thought to be so sacred that no evil could come from them have turned out to be some of the places where the widest and most egregious of crimes have manifest. All of this culminating in the waves that have crashed into our churches, sport teams, and communities with gale force winds. How do we navigate such a storm?

We start with ourselves. We begin this work by going inward and exploring the areas that we have yet to uncover and grow in. This means examining our own biases, reading and listening to voices that make us uncomfortable, and moving through that discomfort on our way to personal evolution. We cannot expect to have an impact on our youth or communities if we have not done this first.

Second, we work in our micro-spaces. Modeling the behaviors we want to see others exhibit, and bringing to light the small ways that we disrespect or are careless in our interactions through our homes and classrooms. The ripple effect of this grows and expands farther than we can see or even image. One life touched becomes a dozen, a hundred, and more. A single interaction, a solitary comment, changes how a child forever thinks about their actions. Peers, siblings, and cousins begin to expect more from each other and correct offensive and unkind words. This conditioning is the spark of cultural change.

Once ignited, the flame grows as the children we taught and raised go out into the world and spread these messages. These children become business leaders, parents, educators, and partners who see consent as central to all that they do. They extinguish the rape culture narratives by speaking up and drawing attention to it as unacceptable—not any longer will they tolerate what others accepted.

By starting to explore the recesses of our own minds, we have created an impact that will outlive us. While this does not mean that violence will no longer be a part of life everywhere forever, it does mean that when something happens, the response is positively impactful. Our goal shouldn't be to change the world to a perfect world but to change it to respond to imperfection productively.

The conversations we are currently having about sexual violence, consent, and gender are both new and timeless. They are discussions long overdue that have never ended. Part of this juxtapose is the fact that while these have remained ongoing dialogues, they have been isolated to only a few communities and spread through limited outlets. In this book you will be given ideas for conversations to have in the classroom and at home as well as information that goes beyond the surface conversations we often have about consent. By going deeper, we can develop within ourselves a greater understanding of what our ultimate goal for creating consent cultures is and how to begin this work by living and modeling it within ourselves.

Through this book you will gain insights into what consent is and is not; know how to facilitate these conversations effectively in your classrooms, homes, and communities; as well as understand the behavioral science behind rape-free cultures and values-based education. We will go on a journey together to uncover more than the 101 version of consent education but also the complex nuances such as internalized bias, cultural scripting, and moving beyond consent in regard to sexual negotiations. We will also explore how culture, gender, and religion play into the beliefs we have internalized unconsciously and how to use these identities to further solidify the importance of consent being for every audience and community. At the end of each chapter you will find a summary of what was covered in that chapter with clear summaries of the key elements to take away.

Thank you for taking this journey with me. I hope that you glean fresh insights from what we explore in the following chapters and that you find tools that you modify and adapt to your homes and communities. You are not alone in your desire to create a culture of consent—together we can move to spaces and paradigms beyond our greatest hopes and dreams.

Chapter 1

Why Consent?

WE DIDN'T KNOW WHAT WE DIDN'T KNOW

Growing up in the southern Bible Belt in the 1990s and early 2000s, tweens and teens were saturated with the purity culture of the evangelical Christian movement. The churches we attended and the media we were allowed to consume (which was very selective and intently monitored) all spoke of sexual chastity until marriage as the ultimate goal in a young Christian's life.

The first messages teens received about sexuality were that it was dangerous and could in an instant spread out of control, like a wildfire. They were told that girls attending the spring pool party had to wear an oversized knee-length T-shirt if they wanted to participate. Girls who wore only a bathing suit, even a one piece, would not be allowed to join in. The imperative for this was clear—they had to protect the boys from sinning.

Every piece of media consumed was closely monitored—from movies to television, and even books read had to get approval and few met the standard. To this day many of those who grew up in this culture still don't understand certain generational media references because they were not allowed to watch or read what our peers were exposed to.

What many of them learned from our youth group leaders, and the courtship books they were allowed to read, was that men were born weak and women were easy targets for their lust. Women were to dress modestly to help boys with their sinful nature, which could, in the worst cases, cause lust to turn into rape. Not only would girls be victims, but they would also have to reflect on what messages they were sending to cause them to act like this. They were told the greatest gift you could give your future spouse was your "purity" and to explain otherwise on your wedding night would break your true love's heart.

Sex itself was fine as long as you were married but even then, procreation and "natural acts" still had to be the focus (no anal, oral, or kinky sex for godly couples). Many of us proudly wore silver purity rings—a stack of three delicate bands saying "true, love, and waits." We were to only take them off for our engagement ring and then a wedding band, a daily reminder that sexual sin was forever a threat and our eternity at stake for it.

So many of us have grown up hearing these messages that we don't look at them critically. We see the overall message as well-intended and excuse the broader implications of these scripts causing any real harm. Many in our evangelical Christian Community went as far as to attend purity balls where fathers and daughters danced, and girls swore their bodies and virginity to their fathers until he and she agreed upon a husband for her.

A study done in 2017, by sociologist Dr. Emily Schafer, showed that seventy of U.S. participants believe that women should automatically change their surname to their husband's and the half of those surveyed believe it should be a legal requirement. The only reasons women's names are changed at all is to demonstrate an exchange of power and property—we go from being our father's possession to our husband's, a factor that is one of the cornerstones of a rape-prone society.[1]

CHANGING THE NARRATIVES

We as a society see a name change, a purity ring, an extra-large T-shirt over a bathing suit and say they mean no harm. But the messages they nurture, if left to fester in the wrong hands, evolve into the foundations that lead to sexual violence, sexual harassment, and domestic violence.

If you have opened this book, you are at least somewhat interested in the concept of affirmative consent. You may have heard about it through personal or professional exposure, be someone who lives by it or simply interested in learning more about what it really means. You may have seen recent news stories promoting the concept with teens and children and felt confused by what it was genuinely trying to promote.

As prevention educators and consent experts we know all too well that many of the stories circulating in the media take consent out of context. They make it seem like we are asking for everyone to be paranoid about every single interpersonal interaction they have. That everything can make a person cry harassment or assault like they are crying wolf, which is in no way what we are promoting or believe in. What we are discussing as a movement and within the pages of this book really boils down to one thing—R-E-S-P-E-C-T.

When we think about the things we want our children to be, the values we want them to share, respect for others is at the top of that list. We want them to live not just by the golden rule, do unto others as you would have them do unto you, but the platinum rule, do unto others as they would ask done unto them.

It is our desire to help them to empathize with the experiences of those around them, but even when they can't connect to someone else's perspective or feelings we want them to honor their requests and needs all while maintaining their sense of self and boundaries. It is within this framework that we find our sincere appreciation for consent. Consent as a concept, as a practice, as a discipline, and a way of living. If consent means anything, it must begin and end with respect for one another's dignity, humanity, and personal autonomy.

MANY QUESTIONS, FEW ANSWERS

We are living in a time when the word "consent" is a word on the tip of so many tongues. Many have embraced it wholeheartedly, while some have reservations and others find offense in its basic tenants. The reason for these variations in reactions is the fact that this entire conversation is so new to the Western world. We didn't grow up with these concepts and hearing that the way we may have joked, been complacent, and overlooked things laid a foundation for the major crises we are observing today can feel far-fetched and extreme. We can't be that bad, right?

As parents we know how much already weighs on us. As teachers we are also well aware that the standards and statutes we are asked to follow can flood our days and already keeps us up at night. To say there is another box to check, another thing to fear, and a new way you are screwing up is not the message we want you to get from this book. In fact, it is quite the opposite.

Our hope is that by guiding you—whether you are a parent, and educator, or concerned and caring member of the community—on this journey you walk away feeling empowered and excited. We cannot hide our heads in the sand or say that this isn't something we have to address because we do explicitly.

Every single day children, teens, adults, and the elderly are sexually harassed, abused, and assaulted. You probably know at least one survivor of this kind of abuse, or you may identify as one yourself. You know this happens and perhaps on a scale far greater than anyone will ever truly quantify. As people who interact with kids and teens, we want to protect them but often feel overwhelmed by the question of *how*. That is why this book was written, to provide some answers and tools to what works and how to lay a foundation for shifting from a culture that fosters abuse to one that eradicates it.

CULTURE AND HISTORY

To understand the current consent movement, we must first understand the history of consent. Around the world for most of human history consent has been minimally applied to wholly ignored. Instead, the standard has been the exact opposite: victim-blaming is the first reaction. We slut-shame women for having healthy sexual desires, we say men/boys have uncontrollable sexual needs and that every guy wants any sex he can get (thus there can't be male survivors).

These messages are sneaky and subliminal. We don't sit down and listen to lectures telling us these myths and lies; instead, they seep into our consciousness through music, media, jokes, and passing comments. Because they aren't blaring, we accept them as "not that bad" and internalize the much larger and more severe messages they give.

Around the world there are wonderful examples of consent culture. These communities are often referred to as "rape-free cultures" by social scientists. Let those words sink in for a second—*rape-free cultures*. Did you ever think of a community or culture as rape-free? Now it is important to note that rape-free culture does not suggest that literally no one has ever been raped in the entire community's history, but rather that rape (and often domestic violence) are incredibly rare (often only perpetrated by outsiders), and that rape as a word or part of life is foreign or unheard of.

Anthropologist Dr. Peggy Sanday has made exploring these cultures and their unique traits the focus of her work. Dr. Sanday has found the following attributes to be consistent across rape-free cultures:[2]

1. **They do not have toxic extremes of gender, especially with boys and men.**

    Rape-prone cultures encourage and enforce women and men to be dichotomous and binary. They socialize girls/women to be submissive and passive and possessions to be owned by men. Boys/men are encouraged to be aggressive and to demonstrate their male identity through interpersonal violence and a lack of emotion and empathy.

2. **Women have an active role in leadership and social discourse.**

    When women and girls are forced to be silent, both literally and figuratively, in all aspects of society or where their voices are seen as bothersome or unimportant, sexual violence increases and is normalized.

3. **Sex is about power and control.**

    Sexual expression, identity, and relations can be viewed through a variety of lenses depending on the culture you grew up in. In rape-free cultures, sex is about interpersonal connection and women are empowered to enjoy sex and speak up about their pleasure and needs. Rape-free cultures generally do not shame out-of-wedlock pregnancies or having multiple partners in a woman's lifetime. Rape-prone cultures make sex taboo and something only men should enjoy, much to the chagrin of their female partners. Women are seen as vessels to be owned and breed to their one and only master—usually passed down from the father to a male he deems worthy of his property.

Before we start to look at that list and think, "Oh, yes what barbaric foreign cultures. I'm so glad I don't live in a society like that," let me remind you that if you are part of a Western or industrialized society, yes, you do. Male dominance and female subordinance are all over our society. From the words we use for sex to how we joke about not letting our daughter date until they are senior citizens, all of these comments and norms are very much part of our rape-prone culture. Take, for example, our cultural obsession with purity.

HOW KIDS LEARN CONSENT

If the first step in understanding why consent is vital is to understand the problem and that it exists, then the second would be to find a way to teach children how to behave according to the new normative frameworks we desire to create. Far too often we are saturated with the woes of the world, shown suffering and tragedy, but never given a solution to act upon. By the time you close this book that is what we wish for you above all—to have a plan to go out and act on what you have learned. To do this, we need to understand how children learn values and scripting.

Jean Piaget was one of the world's first child development and learning theorists. Almost everyone who has taken an education or psychology 101 course will recognize his name and know a bit about his theories. In the 1950s he began to document and write about his observations of how children learn about the world and at what stages of development do beliefs and a sense of self solidify.

One of the first things he came up with was schemas. Piaget defined schema as "a cohesive, repeatable action sequence possessing component actions that are tightly interconnected and governed by a core meaning." So what does that mean? It means that the first foundation of learning is created by observing patterns and categorizing what we see and experiences into neat little boxes. This also has to do with something that is vital to the consent conversation: sexual and social scripting.

Scripting means the predictive pattern of communication that a community follows. For example when someone says, "Hello," you will usually expect to say hello back. Followed by what? Probably, "How are you?" and, "I'm good" or, "Fine, thanks." Your brain has observed this script so many times, and your culture has normalized and expected it so that it has become something you see as unchanging and unambiguous. That is a form of schema and a social script.

Another part of this schema is physical action. When someone waves to our baby, we will often pick up their cute little chubby hand and say, "Wave hello." In the United States, we greet each other with a handshake in formal settings or a light hug in more casual and close interactions.

We don't think about it because we have this physical schema in our mind that was taught to us as babies and toddlers. It is observed all around us even if no one showed us directly and is passed down through each generation. But what does saying "hello" or reaching out your hand to greet someone have to do with sexual consent?

The same way we watch and observe how to greet each other and comply with our culture's scripts in meeting or parting or eating at a restaurant, we also follow these schemas for romantic, sexual, and all inter-person interactions. Children see how parents and other couples speak to each other; they watch how couples dialogue in movies and music. They learn what an expected and accepted way to ask to contact someone you like is, how to show one's love and devotion, and what or what not to put up with.

Without any form of intention, your children have probably already cataloged a large volume of information on sex and relationships—even if they can't define either word yet. Hidden in those files are messages about what love means, what level of respect to expect, and how to treat others if they are seeing examples of one person putting aside their voice and boundaries for another. It's all been cataloged. If they see relationships being a place where autonomy is left to die that has been input, too.

Now, you're probably thinking, "But I tell them differently." I'm sure you do, but the reality is that if you are not actively modeling respect for other, personal agency/autonomy, and consent on a daily basis, then all the words in the world won't change a thing. Please do not think this is meant to shame or guilt anyone in any way. Instead, this is an invitation to increase your awareness—both of yourself and your environment.

Another crucial part of Piaget's theory is the idea of assimilation/accommodation. Assimilation refers to the need to see consistency and accommodation is what happens when that consistency is disrupted, and a new pattern must be organized. For example, if a child sees dogs as big and puppies as small, they think all small dogs of any age are puppies until someone explains that some dogs don't grow to be large even when they are old.

Adults do this kind of thing, too. Many people are unaware of what hair coverings differentiate Sikhs from Muslims. Sadly, this has led to increased violence against both communities and many ignorant remarks to Sikhs who have a completely different faith, deity, and history than Muslims, but also cover their hair.[3] We are all programmed to paint people, situations, and scripts with far too wide of a brush.

These broad strokes create toxic stereotypes which harm not only the victims of prejudice but also those who internalize them; this reality requires that we take a proactive approach in discussing and addressing conscious and unconscious bias with young people at home and at school. We cannot simply hope that children/teens do not pick up on bias attitudes, we must model and have dialogue around assumptions and the harm that they cause.

In consent education, this means that when a young person hears in a song or in a romantic comedy about never letting someone you love go, we must explain, in no unclear terms, how a hyperbolic story or lyric has consequences. The reality being that these behaviors can lead to harassment and stalking charges in real life and cause the object of their affection to feel fear, not infatuation.

It also means that for many parents and educators we must first *unlearn* the messages we have accepted and internalized before we can help the next generation. We see a constant stream of jokes in memes or on social media about women being crazy or dangerous if their male partners step out of line.

Assimilation tells us that a meme is a joke and not something to take literally or be concerned about. Accommodation allows us to learn that while humor may have the intention of not causing harm, the repercussions of learning how these images and messages impact male survivors of domestic violence from reporting or being believed causes us to pause and reconsider.

WHO SHOULD TEACH WHAT?

In reviewing the history of sex education we can see how there has been a long-standing debate over whether or not schools have the right or responsibility to teach such a sensitive topic. Many parents fear that their children will receive inaccurate information or be exposed to beliefs that contradict their own around sex, love, and reproduction.

Certainly, this is a valid concern. Families should want their children to know what they think about anything that intersects with socialization and morality and they should feel included in understanding the topics that are being discussed so that they can continue these conversations at home. Our erotophobic obsession with sex and morality is not logical, is rather uniquely American, and it is hurting our youth.

Parent Educators

Research on the dichotomous attitudes around teen sexuality between Dutch and American parents shows us how important parental communication and education can be in predicting STD and unwanted pregnancy outcomes. A study conducted in 2010[4] looked at the ways that parents in both countries talked to their teens about sex and relationships. In Holland parents saw sex as just another natural part of growing up and becoming an adult. Like with driving or financial stewardship they talked to their teens about sexuality as something to make informed and caring decisions about but not something to fear or blow out of proportion.

Dutch parents preferred that their teens explore sexually within their own homes so that if issues arose their parents would be there to help and make sure everyone was ok. This also meant that the parents knew their children's sexual/romantic partners better, because they were dating openly and, in their homes, and that they could make sure their children had access to safer sex resources.

To the opposite end many American parents preached fear and abstinence. If they did allow any kind of safer sex discussion, they had to preference it with "I don't condone this." These messages meant teens had to sneak around to explore in secret and often did not protect themselves or their partners. This also left them more vulnerable to intimate partner violence and manipulative tactics. American teens had higher rates of STDs, unwanted pregnancy, and similar related outcomes as opposed to their more sex positive counterparts in Holland.

A study published in 2017 examined twelve years of research on parents as sex educators in the United States and what common factors where observed therein. The results showed that children expect their parents to initiate sex education conversations where parents expect their children to ask them the questions, leaving both parties waiting on each other to what to say and when. Findings also concluded that mothers far and above fathers take on the responsibility of discussing sex and that this is almost exclusively framed as a fear-based narrative of preventing worst-case scenarios such as disease, violence, and teen pregnancies.

Most of the parents incited fear of encouraging sexual behavior, lack of subject matter knowledge, and their own bias over past sexual experiences as barriers to comprehensive and ongoing conversations with their children.[5]

Parents should not see schools as taking educational opportunities from them but see them as simply filling in one piece of a very large and complex puzzle. Additionally, sex is not something that just anyone could or should teach. Yes, we all have personal experiences and perspectives to share but like any science there are facts, figures, research, and medical components that require in-depth education and training to fully cover.

As children grow older they need to have certified professionals helping them to understand everything from chemistry to nutrition to sexuality in order to be able to make the most informed and empowered decisions about their bodies and lives. We can teach a bit of chemistry from a book or remember a good amount of our high school Italian to pass on but that does not mean someone is a subject matter expert in either, nor should they be the main authority for our children to learn these subjects.

Additionally, not all parents can teach about sexuality. For some the topic is too emotionally volatile, for others they have had little or no education themselves and may share misinformation, and for others they cannot teach their children about sex because of their own mental illness or abusive behaviors. Of children who are sexually abused in their youth, 80 percent are sexually abused by a parent.[6]

For parents who can and do wish to talk to their children about sex, consent, and violence prevention schools should be on the frontlines of offering education, not only for the students but also for the parents and families. One of our most passionate pleas and suggestions to K–12 schools is not to leave parents behind: most of them want to be armed with resources and information, but also were excluded from these discussions in their adolescent years.

One study that was conducted explored best practices for promoting parent-child conversations around sexual abuse showed that by giving parents education about the prevalence of the issue and ways to facilitate hard conversations. The study's researchers then conducted a follow-up interview with parents showed an increase in conversations started, increases in self-efficacy and response-efficacy beliefs, that is, beliefs around their ability to conduct hard conversations and to cope with questions or disclosures during those talks.[7]

If your school offers sex and consent education, please assure that a complimentary workshop and ongoing resources are offered to parents and guardians. Messages shared at school can be miscommunicated through the filter of children's perceptions, and parents who invalidate or dismiss school messages can invalidate educational efforts.

By assuring that everyone involved in a child's life understands what is being expressed, the learning objectives therein, and how to continue these conversations at home (even when families may disagree or offer their own perspectives), is crucial to building cultures not just classes of consent.

School-Based Educators

Even health teachers must face greater scrutiny in the standards they must meet when teaching about sex. Simply passing your state's health sciences exam does not mean you are ready to face and unpack all of your personal, cultural, and generational biases around sex. Since the early turn of the twentieth century organizations have been trying to unify standards around sex educator certification.[8] Many states allow a number of different certifications to fall into the sex education category—from home economics to physical education to health.

Most of these certification's examinees will require only a passing grade on a test that covers everything from diabetes to HIV and nothing on actual sexology as a scientific field. This means that a teacher could get everyone one of the sexuality questions wrong, have zero interest on touching the topic, and still be certified to teach the course. Other schools will allow a visiting educator to come in and teach about sexuality.

Sometimes it is a nurse who can touch on the medical aspects but may have no comprehensive training on topics such as affirmative consent or gender identity; in other situations, it is someone who the district has assigned to be the closest thing to a sex educator, though they have no formal education or extensive certification in sexology, but are still willing to be seen as the local "expert." And that's only for public schools!

Private schools often have no requirements on sex education, even if their state or district does. This means that all requirements such as medical accurate information or addressing the topics at all can be thrown out the window. Another dimension where this shows up in the worst way is in schools for students with different abilities.

Research conducted in 1971 explored what qualifications sex educators in schools for the deaf had. They found that any teacher of any subject could be assigned the task but that less than 4 percent of the deaf teacher preparation programs ever touched on sexual health education.[9]

One of the most profound experiences in sex educator preparation that a person can have, and that should be required of all sexuality educators in schools, is a Sexual Attitude Reassessment.

This is a two-to-three-day intensive where expert trainers help aspiring educators and therapists explore their biases, beliefs, and ethics about sexuality and working with diverse students/clients. This program forces practitioners to examine what prejudices they have internalized, how their own sex education and early experiences influence them today, and the ways in which they can continue to learn and be culturally humbled.

We cannot accept less than these standards for our children's sex educators. Sexual health education is a human right, according to the World Health Organization and World Association for Sexual Health.[10] Sexuality is a scientific field of study, not an appendage to other forms of medical and social science. We must demand that our children and their communities utilize the experts in this field to insure the best educational experience and long-term outcomes.

In the end sex education will always be an educational tapestry woven between home, community, and schools. This is the purpose and beauty of blending home education with community and school-based education. Children learn from multiple sources creating a holistic perspective on the world around them.

Family traditions, values, and experiences blend with peer-reviewed research and Socratic discussion from peers and teachers alike. Together the students take pieces of knowledge from this collage of resources and formulate their own unique ways of knowing.

IS CONSENT EDUCATION SEX EDUCATION?

As we have just laid a foundation for understanding sex education, its history, competencies, and dissemination, you are likely thinking that consent education is firmly rooted and interwoven with sex education. Allow us to explain another perspective on why it is not.

One of the biggest mistakes we see within consent/sexual misconduct prevention education is that it tends to focus too strongly on consent within sexual situations or only in the bedroom. This leads people to falsely believe that you should only talk about consent when you are ready to talk about sex. Thus, students only hear of the very concept of consent once they are in high school (if they are very lucky) or college during a training on Title IX.

These beliefs are also why many parents and administrators fear discussing consent in school, especially in primary school settings. When parents are asked if they talk to their kids about consent, many will say, "No, not yet, they are too young." Or parents will come and ask when they should start talking about consent with their child. When we reply around eighteen months old they are often taken a gasp.

Consent is absolutely vital to sex. Consent is the line in the sand the separates sex from rape. But consent begins long before sex is ever present and can be completely nonsexual. Consent is above all respect for the dignity, personhood, and well-being of every living thing. It means not simply asking for or receiving permission but holistically seeing each person that you interact with and wanting them to enthusiastically and wholeheartedly choose whether to interact with you or not.

As children this means respecting what your friend wants to play at recess, respecting each other's differences and needs for physical and emotional space. In romantic situations this means respecting if someone doesn't want to text you back without demanding answers and seeking clarification when hesitancy is noticed. Consent is rooted in all interpersonal exchanges, not just sexual ones.

THE HISTORY OF SEX EDUCATION IN THE UNITED STATES

To understand the current to be in sex education in the United States we must first understand its history. Sex education became a part of school curricula starting as early as the late nineteenth century. At that time, its main focus was the prevention of venereal disease and public health. Schools were allowed to cover tools for decreasing disease transmission if nothing else. The first schools to begin these programs were in Chicago. They had some early success with decreasing disease transmission but were quickly shut down by the local Catholic diocese.

In the early twentieth century sex education continued to form into a more organized debate with three schools of thought taking control of the discussion. First, there were the Social Purity Advocates. Social Purity focused on the morality around sex before marriage and making sure that disease and unplanned pregnancy were seen as the dire consequences of not obeying God's natural order for relationships. The Social Hygienists took the stance of all sex education needing to be from a place of public health education. Their only focus was venereal disease with some slight touches on pregnancy and no moral dialogue or discussion of sex outside of public health concerns. The last camp was the Free-Love Radicals. Their ideology was based on the idea that sex was healthy and positive, and that young people simply needed tools in order to experience the benefits of sexuality and love without any of the moral fear mongering.

Looking back at these three early schools of thought we can see the roots of the discussions that we are still having today in the political sex education arena.

Post-World War II saw the second resurgence in sex education being seen as an imperative to public health. Soldiers coming back from World War II brought with them many venereal diseases, something that needed to be addressed if not holistically at least from a health care perspective.

In the 1980s the next wave of concern about protection and sexual morality came in the form of the AIDS crisis. We are still feeling the repercussions from this today. As sex education continues to evolve we see the divergence in outcries for comprehensive discussions that include everything from consent to trauma to pleasure and on the other hand continued foothold in the framework of fear-based and religiously founded abstinence education.

WHAT DO YOU TEACH YOUR
KIDS ABOUT CONSENT?

In the spring of 2019, we designed and disseminated a survey on what parents teach their children about consent. We sent it out through

Survey Monkey and promoted it on social media and through e-mail marketing. The results from the fifty parents who participated were incredibly insightful as to the current conversations progressive parents are having with their children.

The survey questions and responses were as given in figures 1.1–1.6.

The results of this small sampling of parents reflect much of what we see out in the field: parents and educators want to talk about consent, and most do in one way or another. We can see in question 1 that most parents feel that they have addressed consent by talking about respecting people's feelings. We often hear men say that they understand consent because they were taught to "respect women." While this is a start, and very well-intended, it does not adequately address the complexities of interpersonal and gender-based violence. Nor does it do anything to address the violence that boys, men, nonbinary, and transgender people face. The same is true for the response that parents are still sticking to the slogan "no means no."

Yes, we discussed no means no	46.00%	23
Yes, we talk about respecting other's wishes/feelings	68.00%	34
Yes, we talk about not only 'no means no' BUT also 'yes means yes'	28.00%	14
No, not really	6.00%	3

Total Respondents: 50

Figure 1.1   Have You Had Conversations with Your Children about Consent?

Not comfortable, it is overwhelming and/or confusing in today's day and age	0.00%	0
Not comfortable because it concerns pre-marital sex	2.00%	1
Somewhat comfortable	10.00%	5
Very comfortable, I understand this topic in-depth	16.00%	8
Very Comfortable, I know how important it is to talk about even if I don't have all the answers	72.00%	36
TOTAL		50

Figure 1.2   My Comfort Level with the Topic of Consent Is.

No means no	85.42% 41
Yes means yes, enthusiastic consent	43.75% 21
Verbal and nonverbal consent	66.67% 32
Token resistance/compliance	16.67% 8
Communication barriers and obstacles	25.00% 12
Bodily autonomy	64.58% 31
Power dynamics in relationships	39.58% 19
Consent outside of sex	56.25% 27
Cultural influences on sex and consent	20.83% 10

Total Respondents: 48

Figure 1.3 When Discussing Consent I Talk about.

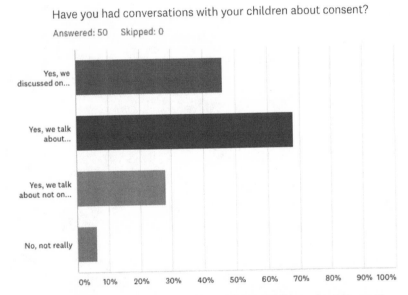

Figure 1.4 Have You Had Conversations with Your Children about Consent?

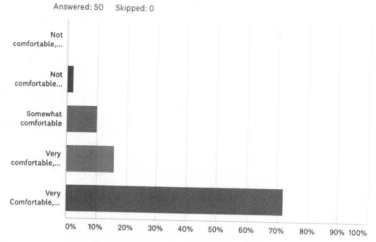

Figure 1.5 My Comfort Level with the Topic of Consent Is.

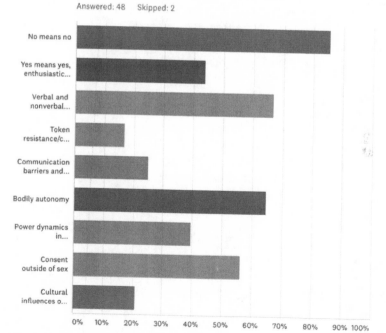

Figure 1.6 When Discussing Consent I Talk about.

The problem then is not that consent is being *ignored* as a conversation that parents are having with their children (very few said they do not discuss it), it is that such a deep and broad topic is often boiled down in ways that do not cover the *most relevant aspects* of this discussion. Should respecting each other and stopping at "no" be a launching point for discussing consent with children? Yes. Should it be the beginning, middle, and end? No.

It is encouraging to see that in question two most parents replied far and above on average that they do feel comfortable talking to their children about consent, even though they may be confused or overwhelmed by aspects of it. This is terrific news because it means that there is an opportunity to continue educating parents and teachers on how to feel better equipped in exploring consent conversations with youth. The greatest obstacle is reaching those who feel uncomfortable with the topic entirely.

Only one parent responded that they feel consent is a conversation about premarital sex and none of the respondents said "no" straight out. The media exposure to the topic is creating a positive ripple effect: parents see that this is something that must be discussed and that they need to start earlier than they previously thought. Even when they know that there are aspects of where consent conversations are going that they don't understand, they still know that having an open dialogue with their children and planting whatever seeds they can offer is better than burying their head in the sand.

The topics that parents are most comfortable talking to their children about regarding consent were "no means no," "bodily autonomy," and "verbal and nonverbal consent." This is consistent with the messages we have received culturally on sexual assault prevention over the past thirty years and mirrors some of the recent conversations we have seen in the media on respecting children's personal boundaries.

The least discussed of the options presented were token resistance/compliance, communication barriers, and power dynamics in relationships. This also was of no surprise to me. Even when working with other prevention educators and victim advocates these are topics they have rarely been exposed to, much less trained on; this is the difference between someone who was training on the job and someone who is a scholar and researcher on a specific subject matter.

Few people will know exactly what tokenism is, much less how it is interconnected with consent. Tokenism is a direct component of

2. Sanday, P. R. (2003). Rape-free versus rape-prone: How culture makes a difference. *Evolution, Gender, and Rape*, 337–362.

3. Verma, R. (2006). Trauma, cultural survival and identity politics in a post-9/11 era: Reflections by Sikh youth. *Sikh Formations: Religion, Culture, Theory*, 2(1), 89–101.

4. Schalet, A. (2010). Sexual subjectivity revisited: The significance of relationships in Dutch and American girls' experiences of sexuality. *Gender and Society*, 24(3), 304–329. doi:10.1177/0891243210368400.

5. Flores, D., & Barroso, J. (2017). 21st century parent–child sex communication in the United States: A process review. *The Journal of Sex Research*, 54(4–5), 532–548.

6. United States Department of Health and Human Services, Administration for Children and Families, Administration on Children, Youth and Families, Children's Bureau. Child Maltreatment Survey, 2016 (2018).

7. Burgess, E. S., & Wurtele, S. K. (1998). Enhancing parent-child communication about sexual abuse: a pilot study. *Child Abuse & Neglect*, 22(11), 1167–1175.

8. Carrera, M. A. (1971). Preparation of a sex educator: A historical overview. *Family Coordinator*, 99–108.

9. Fitz-Gerald, D., Fitz-Gerald, M., & Williams, C. M. (1978). The sex educator: Who's teaching the teacher sex education?. *American Annals of the Deaf*, 68–72.

10. https://www.who.int/reproductivehealth/topics/sexual_health/sh_definitions/en/

https://www.unaids.org/en/resources/presscentre/featurestories/2018/january/20180110_sexuality-education.

Chapter 2

Consent at Home and in School
Why We Need Both

From the moment a pregnancy test comes back positive, we dream of our children's future. Graduations, weddings, milestones—we want them to have it all. Then life hits us, and if we are wise, we take eating this crow pie as a healthy dose of humility. Children come to us with such complicated and confusing personalities. If we have more than one child, we learn what one needs doesn't work at all for the other(s).

Only a few years into parenting we also quickly see that no matter how much we try to protect our precious little ones' hearts and minds, the world around them has equal, if not more, airtime. Other family members, friends, television, the internet, much less school, and extracurricular activities, all take a piece of the pie that forms the values and morals that our children take in.

We want our children to listen to us when we talk about the people we want them to be. Every day we see the competition for their hearts and minds is beyond fierce. We teach them inclusion, but their peers tease and taunt others. We teach them consent is mandatory, but music and movies make a joke of force and manipulation. We tell them gender is nonbinary and that heterosexuality isn't a default identity, but their friends say, "No princess ever married anyone but a prince" in their Disney movies and that anything else is "weird."

The pushback we receive as loving and proactive parents is real and the answers our kids pose will only get harder. As they advance in age, more and more messages seep in that tell them their bodies are consumable, their worth is in proving their "f*ckability," and that to demand respect and mutually satisfying connections is a joke.

We know what that transition into adolescent feels like and may break our hearts to imagine our children being subjected to those lies. The hardest part of this is that we have all grown up with similar messages. Many of us are grateful that we didn't have a smartphone or social media as a teen. Many of us already had low self-esteem and almost zero self-worth as it was. If we had to scroll through feeds telling us we weren't enough, through a medium we had 24/7/365 access to, how would we have survived? And yet, the reality is, that is the world our children are embarking upon.

The hardest part of all this isn't the new challenges, it is the old. The most overwhelming piece of this puzzle is that imagining a world where consent is both sexy and second nature is a world we are just now creating. Often, when we present at conferences, we will ask the audience, "Raise your hand if you grew up in a culture of consent."

Usually we get two to four hands out of a hundred raised. We thank the brave souls who raised their hand, but also take that as a moment to enlighten them. Even if we grew up with the most consent-loving, gender-defying, healthy relationship-having families on earth, we all still grew up in a larger collective culture that promoted the opposite of all of those things. Thus, the battle to overcome these messages is not only for our children to bear but a burden we shoulder right beside them.

The fatigue that comes from realizing how messed up this all is and how hard it is to unlearn it is no easy pill to swallow, but that is where a partnership comes in. You don't have to do this alone. Yes, there are a million entities and individuals out there that want to make these messages sound like mopey liberal hogwash, but there are also forces at work that want to promote these same ideals and change the world for the better alongside us.

That is why schools are at the heart of this journey toward a culture of consent. Our children and their exposure to ethics and morality cannot and should not happen in a vacuum. These topics are too important and take far too much time and energy for parents alone to instill. What is on the line here is no small matter. At large we are trying to change the dynamics that lead to dating violence, stalking, exploitation, harassment, and assault. On a smaller level, we are hoping to change hearts and minds to resist entitlement and toxic gender beliefs and embrace the autonomy.

A quick note on a common misconception about the term "rape culture": rape culture does not mean that everyone in that society will be sexually assaulted and it does not mean that all men are potential perpetrators. It does mean that certain societies are programmed to ignore the continuum that leads to violent attacks and to blame victims when incidents do occur. There are many elements that go into this, which we will explore later in this chapter.

A significant piece of the nurture puzzle rests in our home environment. Even if we are often away from home—at school, with friends, in outside activities—the human mind has deep roots in our family or origin.[1] As helpless as we may feel as parents in the development of our child's moral compass, there is, in fact, a lot of power in how we communicate and model all aspects of right and wrong to our children. Research shows us that, even as teens, children look to their family's values when defining what behaviors they want to emulate. The challenge here is that moral mirroring, or reflecting externally what a child sees at home, depends on family cohesion, adaptability, and positive communication skills.[2]

When working on college campuses we will often interact with parents who are leaving their children in the hands of someone else for the first time. When they hear that the college offers programming for Sexual Assault Prevention and Response (SAPR) they often ask, "Oh, is sexual assault a big problem here?"

The reality is that it is a big problem everywhere. We often then usually ask them what they have told their children about sexual misconduct and affirmative consent. The most common replies are that they put the fear of God in their sons not to get in trouble, that they told their daughters not to be alone with a boy, and for both genders to avoid sex during college.

They usually laugh after saying this. They know all too well that avoiding sex and dating is probably not going to happen, but that is the only thing they can imagine might work. This stance is what we call authoritative parenting. An authoritative moral authority is one that demands obedience, holds rules and standards as inflexible, and does not take into account individual circumstances. This encourages a climate of fear, a lack of honest communication, and an increased likelihood that secrets will be kept, both for victims and for perpetrators.

Another common narrative that comes up in this discussion is that the parents have told their sons to "respect women." Even among athletic coaches and military officials we hear over and over that "be respectful of women" is a major priority and thus sexual violence will therein be combated. This is very well-intended; the people telling me this say so with great pride at their efforts. They firmly believe that seeing women as delicate and vulnerable allows them to be allies in an effective and useful way, but sexism, even benevolent sexism, is always at the root of rape culture.

Here lies the struggle we see at home. Even when parents care deeply about consent and preventing their children from being victims and offenders, they often are not sure what research and best practices even look like. They are walking into a fire blindfolded and covered in gasoline and swear they are trying not to be burned. The good news is that with the right tools they have tremendous influence and power to make a positive impact. Our children are looking to us to define their values and model moral decision-making, but demanding obedience, shaming them for being human—much less sexual beings—or shutting down difficult conversations is not the solution.

As teachers we are often placed in the category of role model, mentor, and sometimes honorary family member. Not every student has the privilege to have parents that care or can take care of their young.

Even when parents are present that may not have the skills to comprehensively discuss certain sensitive topics, and they shouldn't feel like they have to. This plays on "strengths theory," which encourages each individual to hone in on what they already do well, in this case teach well, and to partner with those with complimentary strengths versus trying to become good at something that does not come naturally. In this way each person in the child's life is allowed to run with what they are good at, excelling at their gifts, and the child benefits from receiving a tapestry of information from all of their best resources.

THE CONTINUUM OF HARM

If you are a parent of a child over the age of four, you have probably heard them repeat something you thought they hadn't heard you say (well, hoped they didn't hear you say—oops!). Trust me, we have all been there. Or perhaps they said something beautiful and important that you thought was going over their head and falling on silent ears. Either way, you likely stopped for a moment and marveled at how much these little sponges were taking in from the world around them.

As parents, we are their first world. The sun and moon and stars hang from our heads, at least for a little while. Everything we say or do or believe becomes imprinted on our babies' precious hearts. (As teachers, we often have had a number of colorful conversations with students who assured us we are wrong about a historical or medical fact because "My mommy/daddy says . . . .")

With great power comes great responsibility. While we can argue that we are just people and that our children shouldn't copy everything we do or say, the reality is, at least for the first part of their lives, they will. During adolescence it might feel like our children are off and running away from our example but, again, research has shown us this is not the case.

When it comes to consent, and all of the factors that go into rape-accepting beliefs, home is where the seeds of personal autonomy and empathy or entitlement and apathy are first, and most profoundly, sewn. The challenge here is that even when we care deeply about decreasing sexual and interpersonal violence, we often struggle with effectively modeling these behaviors.

In order to understand what kind of modeling and prevention initiatives work best, we can review a sexual violence prevention theory called "The Continuum of Harm." Most often used by the military's Sexual Harassment and Response and Prevention (SHARP) and SAPR programs, this theory has been used in many foundational conversations concerning the roots of gender-based and interpersonal harm and misconduct. The reason we, as parents and educators, must understand the continuum of harm is that without it violence seems isolated and the causes disconnected from one another, which lead to well-intended but poorly executed efforts.

In the 1980s scholar Liz Kelley coined the term "continuum of sexual violence."[3] This theory has since grown into the term "continuum of harm," though the bases and conclusions of both terms closely mirror each other. The theory goes that cultural norms that make behaviors like entitlement, coercion, trivialization, and emotional violence seen as not-a-big-deal all lead up to assault.

With this in mind, the objective is to address harm before it escalates. Sounds pretty logical, right? The struggle here is that so many early parts of the continuum go unnoticed or excused because they are deeply ingrained in our cultures. How often do we let jokes slide, or say to a victim, "At least it wasn't as bad as . . . ."

We think that if something isn't a huge violent explosive act, then it doesn't deserve as much effort or energy. The continuum of harm seeks to dismantle just that.

The continuum of harm starts at the seeds. What causes the violence and apathy of community violence and serial perpetrators? Does this really come out of nowhere? Do we really not know where these problems begin to germinate? Good news, folks—we do know, and we can address it early on! But it might not be what you think.

The seeds of harm and sexual violence begin in our thoughts and words. Believe it or not, the terms we use for everything from sex to our bodies and gender all add up to cultures that permit and foster incidents like rape and violence. Teens use a variety of different words for sex. Common terms include things like *hitting it, tearing it up, smashing, tapping it, screwing,* and *bumping uglies,* to name a few.

These are the terms young people are hearing all around them, and that isn't likely to change anytime soon. The sooner you accept that and talk about it honestly and in an upfront and open way, the higher the chances that we can explore what terms like these have in common and how they affect our mindset. After reviewing these terms, what do you notice that they have in common? The answer: violence. All of the most popular slangs for sex include aggressive, violent, controlling imagery. We know that impacts how people of all ages approach sexuality and relationships.

The continuum of harm starts in our minds and mouths. In those words, we create subconscious actions that violate boundaries and negate the imperative for consent. The continuum of harm brings to mind a favorite proverb:

> *Be careful of your thoughts, for your thoughts become your words.*
> *Be careful of your words, for your words become your actions.*
> *Be careful of your actions, for your actions become your habits.*
> *Be careful of your habits, for your habits become your character.*
> *Be careful of your character, for your character becomes your destiny.*

When we make sex something to be taken and our partners' bodies something to be owned, everyone loses. Even the way we discuss sexual initiation is about shame and loss. We tell young people, primarily female young people, that they "lose" their virginity. Sex is something that robs you, something that is given away instead of a blessing or gain. This initial fearmongering goes on our whole lives and leads to slut-shaming, respectability politics, and body-policing: all of which end in the worst lie of all—victim-blaming.

WE *ALL* GREW UP IN RAPE CULTURE

Have you ever heard someone say they weren't prejudice? Such as that they "didn't see color" or "didn't have a sexist bone in their body"? Maybe you have even said some of those things at one time or another. It is certainly a nice thought, isn't it? As though if we are just nice enough and have good intentions then bias can't touch us or that we can just wish it away.

The same goes for our participation in rape culture. We like to see the perpetuation of rape-enabling beliefs and ideologies as something that happens outside of us: our actions, our families, our communities. If we are members of marginalized communities or survivors ourselves, we hold this belief especially close to heart. How can I, as the victim of abuse or oppression, possibly be a part of the problem? The answer: internalization.

Even when we have faced bias and prejudice, we also have grown up with the same myths, terminology, and scripting and all of those messages over time have seeped into our conscious, too. We marinade in structural inequality and thus, even with the best of intentions, it becomes part of every one of us.

Gay people have internalized homophobia, women internalize sexism, people of color internalize racism/colorism, and survivors internalize victim-blame. We blame each other for the things we have been taught to hate about ourselves. We monitor our own communities and "keep them in line." We hush the imperfect victims (i.e., sex workers, felons, gender nonconforming folks)—people who are both victims and perpetrators, people who look sound and act less than pure and innocent according to our society's standards.

Where we should sympathize and unify, we build walls and burn bridges. We want to project an image that makes our community look good. Will a drunk stripper getting raped help our cause? Do masculine-of-center women appeal to straight people when we want equality?

Does a trans person who doesn't "pass" as cisgender look good on our promotional materials?

In all of these ways, we shoot ourselves in the foot by not acknowledging the ways in which we are all set up by the system to fail. By identifying this, we begin to find a way forward and use mindfulness to reflect and redirect the negative rape-myth promoting norms we subconsciously perpetuate.

There are two common examples of how insidious consent-violating norms are found in the standards we require young children to follow when it comes to bodily autonomy. One is the way we force children to demonstrate physical affection. When a respected family member or friend is introduced, we are scripted to require that our children greet them with a hug or kiss. This is different than a polite hello or handshake as it places intimate affection as a demand, not agreement. Many children feel shy to show this kind of contact and may have a number of very good reasons for this reservation.

First, they may not feel comfortable with physical touch in general, which is especially true for children with different forms of neurodivergence. Second, they may not feel that they want to have that kind of contact with this person and by demanding it we teach them that certain people who hold particular titles (i.e., grandma, uncle, teacher, priest) must be gifted with our touch no matter our feelings. Third, no matter how closely you watch your children or how involved you are in their lives, no one knows if someone may have hurt them and thus the reason for their discomfort is stemming from something very serious.

We tell our children about the dangers of strangers, and yet statistics show us that the most likely person to sexually or physically abuse a child is a family member or close family friend. Imagining that our baby turns away from a kiss from their aunt because she might have molested them is a deeply disturbing concept. But whether the child is merely expressing a need for physical boundaries or is trying to tell us something far more concerning, the point is that to teach consent begins in these early beliefs and standards.

Explaining to our children, they can wave, say hello, or give a handshake in place of more personal contact reinforces the concept that their body is their own, that no one "deserves" intimacy, and that their voice matters. All of which are the building blocks for sexual and interpersonal consent.

The second example of a common consent-violating norm begins on the playground. When we play with a child, do we listen to what they say? Do we teach them not only to share with others, but that they can set boundaries and respect the physical space of those around them? Everyone has heard a parent say to a child "sharing is caring," but what about saying "ask if it is okay" and "they said no, which means you have to stop."

Numerous consent educators point to the example of tickle play. Whether between adults and children or child to child, tickling is a very intense and physical interaction. Some people enjoy a gentle tickle play, but others find it uncomfortable, and everyone can find too much tickling annoying or even painful.

Many times, when being playful, adults will tickle a child without respecting their physical boundaries all in the name of "fun." A child may start by laughing, but then start to say "stop, stop," only to be met with more tickling and mocking at the child's pleas for a break.

Many adults will say that this is all in good fun and no one is hurt by tickling, but let us really examine what messages are being planted here:

1. If I think you are having fun or enjoying something, then your verbal "NOs" or requests to stop are invalid.
2. Not all "NOs" mean "no."
3. Bodily autonomy is negotiable if I think it is funny.

These messages are part of the continuum of harm, and they translate into dating and sexual consent as a child grows older. If we teach a child that we stop as soon as they say so or seem uncomfortable, even nonverbally, and to identify this in others, then we are raising consent-conscious children.

Adults can begin teaching children about physical consent around eighteen months old. At that age a child can first understand the word "no" and respond (somewhat) appropriately. Teaching a toddler consent means teaching them to understand when someone is uncomfortable and that all parties involved deserve to feel safe and comfortable. One example is respecting their playmate's boundaries. If a child needs space and turns away from playing, the other needs to be told, "They don't want to play right now/that way, let's find someone else or something else to do."

This goes beyond not hitting to reading someone's verbal and non-verbal cues. This can even be translated into playing with animals. When a child wants to pet an animal, we set appropriate boundaries such as telling them not to grab or hit it; however, it goes beyond it: we must teach them to pay attention to whether the animal wants to be touched at all, and if not, how to accept that disappointment and not take it personally. Saying, "The puppy is turning away; she doesn't want to have her belly rubbed." And if the child protests that they want to still pet their soft fur, explaining that the puppy's fur is their own, it is up to them to decide if we pet them or not. If we honestly digest the entire concept of consent, we see that these are the foundational pieces of awareness and respect that will create either cultures of consent or cultures that accept rape-myths.

A large part of the rejection seen from parents and teachers is cognitive dissonance at the idea that their way of being raised could ever be part of the much larger problem like sexual violence. Many adults will say that they grew up with these same standards and narratives and never assaulted anyone. How dare this book (or this author) suggest that these are related?

It would certainly make my job as an advocate and consent educator so much simpler if the only task at hand was to tell people not to assault each other. It is also true that tickling and raping someone are not the same thing *at all*. Please do not think that we are trying to put them on the same plain. What we are saying is that these small messages and lessons do defuse into more significant problems over time and that the only effective way to prevent violence from being excused, accepted, or normalized is to nip it in the bud.

THE MEDIA

Many of us grew up with the ritual of Saturday morning cartoons. Every Saturday we would jump up at the crack of dawn with a bolt of energy and excitement (Remember waking up like that?). We would grab some cereal or a snack, head to the TV room, and plant ourselves in front of a constant stream of colorful animated characters. Many of us weren't allowed to watch much television, so this time was golden. We just couldn't wait to immerse ourselves in the magical fantasy world.

Most people would say that cartoons are a relatively safe space from the rape-acceptance myths that we have discussed so far, but others will now be reviewing the ones they have watched and see some concerning trends. Let us start with some classic cartoons, *Pepé Le Pew*, for example.

Pepé was a skunk who was obsessed with a cat. He chased her down, followed her wherever she went, and no matter how much she protested, he believed deep down she wanted him back and would succumb to his advances eventually. As kids, we laughed at this all in jest. That poor cat, we said, but that's part of being crazy in love.

Notice the description of Pepé: he was *obsessed*, not lovestruck. Because now we know better than to confuse obsession and power and control with romance and love. As children, we ingest those narratives and say he means no harm—but what is really going on with Pepé? He is stalking, harassing, and assaulting that cat. She is a victim, and he justifies his desire and culture as a "French romantic" for his actions.

Looking at many classic fairy tales and Disney movies, we see the same troubling troupes. *Beauty and the Beast* is an example of Stockholm syndrome, where a victim sympathizes and then identifies with their abuser. The Beast was trying to kill her Dad, for Pete's sake! Belle negotiated a hostage exchange and then magically a few months later, "He's changed."

In both *Sleeping Beauty* and *Snow White*, a nonconsensual kiss is what saves them from a living death. The Little Mermaid is a minor who has to give up her voice, family, and identity to live happily ever after. The list goes on and on, and these are only the cartoons we grew up with. Now I'm not saying you have to ban Disney from your life, but we do need to look critically at the messages these stories tell our children and have these conversations with them.

As we get older, the stories stay the same. In the best-selling book and blockbuster movie *Twilight*, a teenage girl is stalked by a geriatric vampire. His inability to communicate and indecisiveness is her ultimate aphrodisiac. She then has to decide between an elderly vampire and a werewolf, who comes from a family of domestic abusers who simply "can't control their rage" at their partners. Great choices, Bella. If only your parents were discussing consent and healthy boundaries with you instead of turning a blind eye to the clear signs that you are scared and imprisoned in your relationships.

The *Twilight* franchise is only one example. Almost every romantic comedy follows similar sexual scripting: partner A wants partner B, partner B ignores or doesn't appreciate partner A, partner A does everything in their power to persuade them—including lying about their identity/motives, following them around, using private information to convince them—and if all else fails, to beg until partner B takes pity on them.

Sounds about right, doesn't it? "But it's cute and funny, and no one gets hurt," you protest. Let us look critically at the behaviors that are being promoted: ignoring someone's verbal and nonverbal "NOs," manipulation, fraud, harassment, stalking, and emotional blackmail/ guilt. The entire premises is based on a "no meaning maybe" and that you can wear someone down and pressure them into liking you.

These are all behaviors that we see repeated in real life (often with Title IX/sexual misconduct offenders). In real life what was cute and sweet on a screen is now terrifying and traumatic for the victim. The offender doesn't understand, they had such good intentions, this couldn't be that big of a deal, until the police show up at their door.

Sexual violence plays out in other ways on screen when the victim is male. Male victims are consistently used a punch line in many mainstream television and film comedies. From *South Park* to *American Horror Story*, *Orange Is the New Black*, *Black Mirror*, and the *Scary Movie* franchise, the idea of a man or boy being anally raped or forced to have sex with someone is still seen as fair game. Where sexual assault of a woman has died down as a humorous concept, male sexual abuse is still seen as a punch line. We, as a society, hypersexualize men just as much as girls, perpetuating the myth that all men/boys want all sex and that male victims are not damaged in the ways that female ones are. This is a *lie*.

After having worked with a number of male victims, we can say, unequivocally, that their pain and trauma are just as real and valid. If we made jokes about female prison rape the way we do about male prison rape, there would be a resounding uproar (and rightfully so). The hit show *Black Mirror* began its series with an episode about a man who is forced to rape a pig. He too was raped by "forced-to-penetrate" assault.

Few people realize that male victims can be stimulated sexually without their consent and then victim-blamed for their arousal by predators and legal systems alike. This is a trauma so deep and so profound. The penis reacts to stimulus the same way a woman cannot control being forcefully penetrated or impregnated. It is not a choice, it is a bodily reflex that leaves men and boys vulnerable their whole lives. If a sci-fi show had started out with an episode about a woman who is raped by an animal on live television, it would have been canceled then and there. We normalize all of these myths and even when we tell ourselves we know it is just fiction, these images imprint on our beliefs, which spread into our legal and social standards.

This is in no way meant to be a media-shaming message. Media allows us to share many valuable and morally sound messages with our students and children. We can watch and discuss historical events, observe and discuss the ways that people are treated in movies and musical lyrics, and watch examples of the kinds of interpersonal dynamics we do want to see in the world around us.

The problem is mindless consumption. The fact is we often are so busy and buzzing around that we turn on the radio, TV, or computer and let something play without ever stopping to think about the messages we are internalizing subconsciously. My advice is not to stop using media but to blend a mindfulness practice, in our homes and classrooms, with what both we and the young people in our life are being exposed to. Taking the examples above here are some ways to start discussions about media:

Pepé Le Pew:

- What does Pepé seem to think about the cat's reaction to his advances? Do you think he is listening to her?
- How does the cat feel? Is she scared/upset/frustrated?
- Do you think sometimes people think they can convince someone to like them if they just try hard enough? Why wouldn't that be a good idea? What could he do instead (find someone who likes him back, not be desperate for affection, respect boundaries)?

Belle, Snow White, Sleeping Beauty, Ariel:

- The Beast seems to really hurt Belle: separating her from her loved ones, controlling where she can go, yelling at her. Do you think if someone treats you like that that you can change them by being nice? *Discuss the cycle of abuse and power and control.*

- Both Snow White and Sleeping Beauty hardly knew the princes they married. Why would someone who feels isolated, like they were, maybe want to get married quickly?
- Should you kiss someone who is sleeping? Especially if you don't really know them?
- Ariel has to give up her identity and family to be with her prince. Do you think people should give up something or who they are to be in relationships? What could they do instead?

Twilight

- Edward is all grown up, he has lived many lifetimes, and Bella is a teenager just trying to figure out who she is for the first time. How can this impact how much power and agency they each have in their relationship?
- Edward comes in and out of Bella's life, rarely with her consent, even appearing in her room at night. Why might a teenager think this is romantic? How is this emotionally manipulative?
- Jacob has an explosive anger issue. Bella thinks she can say and do the right things so he doesn't physically abuse her like the other guys in his family have done to their partners. Do you think many people blame themselves when someone abuses them? Do people often think they can behave "just so" and they won't be hurt? Do you think people with domestic violence in their families sometimes use it as an excuse to do the same; that is, "This is just the way we are?" or, "I've seen worse; I'm not that bad."

WHERE SCHOOLS COME IN

While a child's time at home and outside of a classroom is by far the majority, the classroom hours are nothing to scoff at. We have discussed what goes into creating homes that create environments of consent:

1. Open communication between parents and children. This includes being able to disagree without an automatic punishment and flexible rules and perimeters.
2. Modeling healthy relationships and friendships that follow affirmative consent standards.
3. Talking about the media and how culture shapes our beliefs.

So if those are our goals and objectives for at home, where does school come in? If parents are teaching their children these things, can't we just make school about reading, writing, and arithmetic? Sex educators hear that argument a lot.

Here is the first problem with the "home-is-best" belief system: not all homes are created equally. Saying that every home comes with parents or guardians who are competent to overcome social scripting, personal bias, and understand all of the social theories and standards that go into creating a cultural shift (and it is a significant shift) is simply wrong. To say this is to say that every "good parent" must be born into a certain standard of privilege.

Not all parents are concerned about these topics. Many believe that everything in this book is just a big old pile of propaganda. They do not think that the things college campuses are teaching about consent are true. "Boys will be boys," "Slutty/stupid girls get what's coming," and "You can't change human nature," they'll say.

That is only one example of why not every home can teach consent. There are also those with parents who are dealing with domestic violence, incest, and addiction. There are healthy parents who simply hardly have time to see their children for a meal, much less a long, in-depth conversation because life and finances have forced them to work two or three jobs.

To then say, "Hey, this is on you, time to teach your kids everything about navigating sexual and personal relationships," is both unfair and unrealistic. Additionally, research shows us that of children who are sexually abused 80 percent of the time they are abused by a parent,[4] showing once again that this education must be coming from multiple complimentary sources.

In 2011 when the White House sent out their "Dear Colleague" letter outlining new requirements for schools to teach consent, gender equity, and bystander interventions under Title IX, they sent it to the colleges, not to every parent's home. Schools can be held to the standards of the messages and conduct they expect from their students, the government cannot and should not monitor that in every household.

The problem with only colleges getting these mandates from the government is that by the time young people set foot on campus, eighteen years of opportunities have passed by and social norms have already become ingrained. When working with students who have violated sexual misconduct policies, the first question we ask is, "What did you learn about consent or healthy boundaries growing up?" About half say nothing and the other half will say that they were told that as long as they didn't hold someone down while they screamed "no," it was all theirs for the taking.

Title IX is a gender equity law that most people know as "that college sports thing" or "that rape prevention law for colleges." Very few realize that Title IX applies from kindergarten through graduate school. This means that by not giving students resources and education around these topics, K–12 schools are not living up the Title IX federal guidelines and are prime for the next big hit from the Office of Civil Rights. Age-appropriate education about consent, sexuality, freedom from harassment, and dating violence are all the rights of every young person who steps foot into a school building.

Schools have known since their creation that they are the foundation of nurturing communities and growing productive and responsible citizens, and what is more vital to the objective than the prevention of sexual abuse, domestic violence, and gender equity? Together schools and parents can form alliances that uproot rape cultures and create fertile ground for cultures of consent.

TAKEAWAYS FROM CHAPTER 2

- Most people have the intention of modeling and speaking to mutual respect in relationships but don't know what else they should say—especially to kids.
- The continuum of harm teaches us that assault and violence do not come out of the blue.
- By bringing awareness to what we say and think we can effectively combat rape culture.
- We have all grown up in rape culture: a culture that makes behaviors that violate person and sexual autonomy normative.
- The media does an excellent job at creating social norms—for better or worse.
- By identifying aspects of rape culture in our lives, homes, and communities we can address it head on.

- Schools and parents must partner in order to have a shot at effectively educating youth on consent. K–12 settings are the best time to begin this dialogue as youth are exploring their values and morality.
- College is too late to begin discussing sexual violence and dating abuse.

NOTES

1. Bradley, R. H., Corwyn, R. F., Burchinal, M., McAdoo, H. P., & García Coll, C. (2001). The home environments of children in the United States Part II: Relations with behavioral development through age thirteen. *Child Development, 72*(6), 1868–1886.

2. White, F. A., & Matawie, K. M. (2004). Parental morality and family processes as predictors of adolescent morality. *Journal of Child and Family Studies, 13*(2), 219–233.

3. Kelly, L. (1988). *Surviving Sexual Violence*. Oxford: Polity Press.

4. United States Department of Health and Human Services, Administration for Children and Families, Administration on Children, Youth and Families, Children's Bureau. Child Maltreatment Survey, 2016 (2018).

Chapter 3

Entitlement, Boundaries, and Personal Agency

PRIVILEGE, ENTITLEMENT, AND IDENTITY

Every person on earth is born with certain inalienable rights. One of the most foundational is the right to personal autonomy: autonomy which includes body, mind, and spirit. This means that no matter our age, race, religion, social status, or identity we have the right always to be treated with dignity and respect—from the cradle to the grave.

This means that no one ever has the right to violate our autonomy over our body or mind. No matter another person's status, power, or privilege no one can neither own another nor should they be controlled by another. Now, this does not mean people, especially children, get to live without rules, but that rules and laws should protect each individual's personhood not take from it. Personal autonomy is the marrow of consent; without it, we have no power.

We exist within so many systems that make power and control over others seem normal. Things that no two adults could do to each other are allowed when done to children. Things your boss couldn't do to their employees a teacher can do to students. As parents and teachers, we filter everything we do through these lenses and help our students and children to explore what they find to be unreasonable or unfair as well.

For example, when designing the class rules for the year we should allow the students to spearhead the discussion. As the person tasked with keeping them safe and assuring, we comply with federal, state, and institutional rules, we are there to give suggestions and explain when something they suggest can't be accommodated.

Ultimately, the students are taking responsibility for the class and what needs to be in place for a productive and enjoyable learning environment. This is vital to self-efficacy and personal responsibility. If we come in and tell them what to do, they feel controlled and will want to wiggle away from our grasp. If we are a community and agree together, they accept the standards we mutually agreed to. In addition to student expectations we agree to teacher expectations.

We allow them to ask from us the same that we ask from them. As teachers we are leaders, as leaders we are there to serve. Our students know that we will agree to certain guidelines that their teachers must follow—such as never holding a grudge against any of them and providing clear communication on assignments.

As parents we make sure to not only tell our children how we feel about their behavior but ask them how they feel about ours. We should have regular talks where we set aside time to give each other praise; going around the table and tell one another what we like and appreciate about each person. We also ask them how we are doing as their parents, and if there are ways, we can be better or help them differently.

Giving them this space, without fear of consequences or rejection, to be honest with us, is powerful. Imagine if everyone in your life, who has or currently holds power over you, asked you to tell them how to be better and then acted upon that feedback.

Imagine if these kinds of power dynamics were implemented in every area of society: if the police, judges, and public service officials regularly asked for feedback on their performance with the communities they served—if they asked without threat of punishment, without performance, but with sincerity, only listening not correcting or justifying and then providing action steps for how they would take that feedback and demonstrate improvement.

We have long observed that students only get angry or despondent when they feel unheard. Organizational psychology has found this to be true in employee retention and development. Communities rise up, revolt, and become violent when they feel their leadership is disregarding their needs and voices.

Power and control over others may seem normal in many situations; hierarchies are so ingrained into our culture that we think there is no other way. Thus violence, abuse, and manipulation in macro- and micro-interpersonal dynamics seem to be just a part of life. This is simply not true.

Consent and sexual violence are both topics that are encapsulated in power dynamics. Sexual assault takes away power from one person and gives it to another and consent requires an equal sharing of power. This is why someone who has power and control over another, that is, a teacher, a correctional officer, a boss, cannot receive consent from someone who is a subordinate to them. With our children and youth, this means remembering that they have the same rights as an adult to say what they are comfortable with, ask for space, and feel safe in their body, and all without threat or manipulation.

CHILDISM

The reality is that most societies do not practice this. Instead they practice childism. Childism is akin to racism, sexism, ableism, and so on. It is the belief that because of someone's status they are naturally less than and denied the rights given to another. Childism says that children are not to be believed, should not be given choices, and that trauma incurred is somehow less impactful than if it happened to an adult.

Childism says adults know what is best because they are wiser—the same way men think that women are irrational or how white people will say a black person is naturally angrier and louder. These are all lies we are fed from birth by our culture, so much so that we exist and intertwine with them without ever even noticing. We tell ourselves, "This is just the way it is."

Part of this blindness comes from our privilege. "Privilege" is a volatile and prickly word these days. Many people have a knee-jerk reaction of repulsion when they hear it, but that is simply because it is often very misunderstood. When the world gives us status we didn't earn, and which grants us access, safety, and resources denied to others, we are privileged.

We don't think we deny children their right to affirmative consent because we live in a world where this is normative. We say, "Being an adult is hard, we aren't privileged," the same way a white person says, "I have lived a hard life, I'm not privileged." But we are privileged, even when we face challenges, because those challenges are neither caused nor enhanced by our identity, in this instance, our age.

Take, for example, the progress that has been made in sexual harassment prevention and awareness. We have done so much in the past thirty years, much less the previous two, in this arena. We are talking about how comments, jokes, and unwelcome physical contact can make for a hostile environment and violate that inherent right for personal safety and bodily autonomy. But do we apply this to children and teens?

Many of us grew up accepting that in middle school and high school (and even elementary school) we would be sexually harassed. This is true for people of all genders but especially women and trans/gender-nonconforming youth. Boys would snap the girls' bra straps as early as fourth grade; they would tell each other to "suck it," as a snarky and common remark; and girls were told if they dressed provocatively, they were asking to be sexualized. Now imagine any of that in the workplace today. We, as adults, would never tolerate it.

If your teammate snapped your bra you would report him, if someone made a lewd remark you would call attention to it, and if someone said your work clothes made you fair game for objectification you would discuss it with human resources; all rightfully so. Why then do we think this impacts young people any less?

Childism is the bias and prejudice we have against children: their bodily autonomy, legal rights, sense of identity and expression, believing that children are owned by their guardians, and thus denied basic human rights in many forums.[1] We think that if something happens to a child it is somehow going to have less of an impact: "They won't remember this."

We think that when a child discloses abuse, they must be imagining it or blowing it out of proportion. The reality is while adults make false reports of sexual violence approximately 5 percent of the time,[2] children only false report 1 percent of the time.[3] Trauma from childhood has the longest lasting and most detrimental effects including increased rates of unemployment, drug use, suicide, cancer, and future violent victimization.[4] If there is any age group that should be educated, empowered, and protected from unwanted comments, touch, and attacks it is children and teens.

As parents and educators, we are on the frontlines when it comes to planting the seeds of change in young people's lives. So many people go to work every day wishing they were doing something to make the world a better place. They see problems on the news and are frustrated with the direction things are going but they spend their waking hours having to be separated from the people that need help the most.

They say, "I wish I felt like there was something I could do." As teachers we never have to say this. Yes, there are frustrating limitations and endless red tapes that often feel like they are tying our hands behind our backs from what we could truly accomplish. Yet, every day we spend precious time with the next generation of our society, planting seeds, and never knowing how many of our ideas will germinate and flourish where we least expect it.

As parents we also feel the limitations of our time and energy. We may ask ourselves if we have said enough, explained enough, tried as hard as we could. Our children are watching and listening, even when we aren't speaking to them directly. Our power to influence and encourage them for the better is far greater than we can often recognize.

What a blessing to be interwoven into the fabric of a child's life. Whether a thousand children, or one, we are part of the change and that is a battle already won in and of itself.

WHAT DO HEALTHY BOUNDARIES LOOK LIKE?

Every living thing has boundaries. Physical and emotional boundaries are what allow us to see where we begin, and where another ends. It gives us the space we need to feel safe and to understand what we do and do not feel comfortable with. Without boundaries we are violated, feel insecure, and are in a constant state of hypervigilance. As crucial as boundaries are, we often find ourselves, throughout our lives, having these boundaries violated.

This leads to a state of constant stress and fatigue and can cause stress-related illness and disease. The problem is that even though we know this, we are often conditioned to let people invade or dismiss our boundaries and rarely see helpful examples of people setting healthy boundaries.

The partner who never says "no" to their beloved's every need, the parent who no longer has a personal life, the teacher who works more than seventy hours a week because they care are all socially praised. These poor people have no to few boundaries, are constantly stressed and burned out, and yet are lauded as selfless and sacred. This has to stop. It has to stop for us, and it has to stop for the next generation.

In order to stop these unhealthy cycles and create new norms, we must begin by modeling this behavior. Our children are sponges; they will copy, repeat, and exemplify what they see the adults around them do and say. When our behaviors don't match our words, our children follow what we do. The whole "Do as I say not as I do" thing never works. Here are a few examples of modeling healthy boundaries and consent:

- Your boss calls during dinnertime. They tell you they need you to come in extra early and update your notes even though they aren't due for a week. You need to sleep, and you need to stick to the schedule you have of dropping off your children that day. You tell your boss you understand they want it done tomorrow but that you will do your best to complete it at the previously agreed to time because tomorrow morning you already have previous commitments.

  You modeled healthy professional boundaries and work-life balance. You also showed that you could say no and not consent to a request even from someone in power.

- When you lean in to kiss your partner in front of your children you wait for them to lean back toward you. You make sure you touch your partner in ways that are well-received and welcomed. You ask each other if it is a good time to discuss a topic before approaching a sensitive subject and allow each other space when tensions are high.

  You are modeling consent in your words, actions, and physical contact.

- Your student is upset and acting both tearful and angry. You approach their space slowly, kneel down to their level, and ask if they want to talk. They say they don't know if they do and start to cry. You ask them if they can talk with you outside and they agree. They keep crying, and you reach out your hand and ask if you can give them a hug. They say, "Ok," but shrug their shoulders inward, so you say, "It's ok, you don't have to want a hug, I just want you to know I'm here for you," and give them more physical space.

  You ask them if they would like to call home or see a counselor and they agree. You got consent for verbal and physical interactions. When their body language and words did not match up, you noticed and took the lack of enthusiasm as a lack of consent. You empowered them to make choices and not feel forced to do anything.

- You were up all night talking to your mom who is battling cancer; things are not looking good, so you got only a few hours of broken sleep. You come to the classroom with the weight of the world on your shoulders, and your students notice. You are trying to focus on work and being present, but this is affecting you more than you thought. A student you have been working with is acting up again.

You usually are good at redirecting her, but today you feel that this is getting on your exhausted last nerve and you are going to get visibly angry. You tell her that you know she is trying her best, but you need her to try just a bit harder today, you need her to work with you extra hard to not disrupt the class. She knows you pretty well by now and asks if something is wrong and you tell her you are having a hard time today and you feel depleted. You request that she try to be a little quieter and cooperative and she agrees.

You modeled being human and appropriately having needs. You showed that everyone's physical and emotional boundaries will change and shift and that asking for extra or different support is healthy. You explained that people could ask for this without being rude or aggressive but by communicating and feeling respected.

Consent requires boundaries to exist, be acknowledged, and be respected. Most often we think of the physical boundaries of consent: "Can I hug you? Is this ok? Does this feel good?" Consent begins with our emotional boundaries. One of the first things we notice when we work with young offenders is that they completely disregarded the emotional boundaries of the victim long before they violated anything physical.

In crimes, such as harassment and stalking, physical boundaries sometimes were never violated in a literal sense, though the emotional violation fed into a feeling of physical threat. For example, a young person who continually texts the object of their affection despite this person's unwillingness to respond or clear requests to lessen/stop contact has made the person they are trying to communicate with fear for their physical safety.

On the other hand, someone who has physically assaulted someone first had to ignore that person's emotional boundaries and disregard their mental and physical well-being. Most incidents of stalking and harassment escalate from emotional to a physical violation. Once boundaries are crossed, it only gets worse: the victim loses more and more sense of security and agency, and the perpetrator feels more and more entitled and emboldened. This is why we must begin by teaching the importance of defining and respecting our emotional borders before we discuss physical boundaries, much less sexual ones.

A number of political pundits and conservative bloggers have made light of this by responding to everything they don't like discussing with the retort "I don't consent!" They find it humorous and ridiculous to imagine a world where everything should be consented to. These pundits believe that this means literally demanding verbal consent every time you interact with another person—making a mockery of a legalistic framework for the consent paradigm.

This is completely ignoring the actual message of consent and encouraging their followers to dismiss the topic all together on the claim that it is a ridiculous notion of oversensitivity. If you take nothing else from this entire book, please retain this: Consent is not overly sensitive, politically correct, fodder. Consent is the foundation for civility, human dignity, decency, and the creation and retention of a safe and equitable society. That is nothing to laugh at.

PERSONAL AGENCY: SEXUAL AGENCY, SEXUAL SUBJECTIVITY

We cannot have discussions about consent without exploring the concepts of "sexual agency" and "subjectivity." While these are two terms that the majority of people have not heard before they are so crucial to consent that without them there is no foundation to build a consent culture upon.

- *Sexual agency is the ability to make sexual choices according to one's will, free from coercion. Experiencing oneself as a sexual agent means feeling in control of one's sexual decisions and experiences (Pittard & Robertson, 2008).*[5]
- *Sexual subjectivity: entitlement to sexual pleasure from oneself, entitlement to sexual pleasure from a partner, sexual self-efficacy in achieving sexual pleasure, and sexual self-reflection (Horne & Zimmer-Gembeck, 2005).*[6]

There is fantastic research and discourse on these two frameworks to explore further, but before we understand them theoretically, we must first examine our personal relationship with them. By beginning with the exercise of sitting and digesting these two definitions and how we relate to them personally, we can create a platform to begin working from. These are colossal paradigm-shifting concepts for most of the world and for much of human history so acknowledge that this will take time and should be done mindfully.

Imagine, with me, for a moment that you grew up, went through puberty, discovered your sexuality, and became your true self in a world that gifted you with sexual agency and sexual subjectivity.
Ask yourself this:

- How would puberty have been different for you if you were told that your sexuality was yours alone? That sharing your sexuality, in every aspect, was something that you had the power to navigate and was never taken from you.
- How would your teen and young adult years have been transformed by being told that personal sexual pleasure and mutual pleasure with a partner were your rights?
- What would the impact have been on your early sexual experiences if you were taught how to advocate for and understand your personal and mutual sexual pleasure needs?
- How does mutual sexual and emotional pleasure intersect with enthusiastic consent?
- How would having agency over your sexual expression, free from shame, have changed your ability to advocate for yourself in romantic, professional, and other interpersonal relationships?
- How would opportunities to personally and communally reflect on sexual experiences, both solo and partnered, have impacted your feelings about your body and your rights?

Some of those questions might have hit you hard, and others might have meant very little to you. Take note of those feelings and reflect on how those emotions may ring true for you today. Whether parents or teachers, we are all adults living with the blessings or scars of our early sexual experiences.

Sexual experiences include our response from caregivers when we had questions, our body image, solo sex (masturbation) experiences, and early sexual partners and identity. If those experiences were good, we likely have many fond memories and positive perceptions of sex and ourselves to this day. If we had less-than-pleasant experiences, we might still struggle with finding our sense of agency and subjectivity in this most intimate of contexts.

Research is here to guide us and reflect back what we may individually know or collectively deny with a filter of scientific theory and proof. We cannot deny that what we, as children, teens, and young adults, are told about sex and sexuality will follow us for the rest of our lives. Lives lived in shame and guilt about something that is just as natural as eating or breathing is a burden few can carry well. In the sexual subjectivity research cited before, we see what the benefit of adolescent sexual experience can be.

As Horne and Zimmer-Gembeck point out, "Sexual behavior may provide opportunities for adolescents to develop positive self-esteem and achieve mastery of some developmental tasks, such as the formation of intimate relationships and identity. In the few previous studies of these possibilities, sexual experience, especially early sexual intercourse debut, was expected to be associated with lower rather than more positive wellbeing, and usually the measure of well-being was self-esteem. Results of these studies provided contradictory information."

Their research looked at numerous dimensions in sexual agency and sexual subjectivity. In sexual agency alone they examined how well a subject was able to overcome self-silencing behaviors and resiliency to sexual double standards. The participants were all young women aged sixteen to twenty years old.

What the researchers found in measuring these qualities of adolescent sexual well-being was extradentary: they found that the earlier a young woman had consensual sexual experiences (age sixteen or younger), whether it included intercourse or not, she showed a greater sense of being able to communicate her needs and less likelihood of believing sexual double standards, measures which had been connected to self-esteem and rates of depression. This was also true for young women who masturbated.

We spend so much time and energy fearing our young people, especially our girls, will want to have sex and be sexually agentic beings. The reality is that having sexual experiences that are desired, consensual, and that address each person's well-being increase a teen's ability to communicate their needs, set boundaries, like themselves, feel positive, and reject toxic double standards. Sex is not the enemy and should not be feared, and only honored and respected for the powerful gift it is.

Research tells us that one in three girls and one in six boys will be sexually abused by the time they blow out their candles on the eighteenth birthday.[7] For those children, who are now adults, sexual agency and subjectivity were something denied them from a very early age. While we cannot prevent all abuse and assault, we can reinforce the tools that help survivors speak up, decrease victimization, and provide tools for healing. There is no better place to start than by giving the gift of a world that promotes sexual agency and sexual subjectivity.

CONVERSATION TOOLS AND OUTLINES

Now that we have laid a foundation for bodily autonomy, privilege, power dynamics, and sexual agency we can move into a place where we look for ways to discuss these topics in real-life situations. We will break down conversation starters for each topic by age group and at home versus at school. You can use these to begin working with your students and children but remember that they are simply suggestions and should be modified to each audience, whether it be for one child or a whole classroom.

Be cognoscente that there is no full script because you want to plant the seed but let the development be organic. Try not to overly direct that conversation but offer further questions that help the child come to their own conclusions. You may be surprised at how each child's perspective and inquiry force you to rethink and reexamine your own thoughts and beliefs. The key is to make conversations about consent as natural as possible and infused into daily life and other complimentary topics, not a stand-alone sit-down talk that is siloed or seen as intimidating.

Bodily Autonomy

Age seven and under:

- *Ask your friend if they would like a hug. They didn't say yes, that's ok, let's just wave goodbye.*
- *When can someone touch us without asking first? Never, that's right. What if they are someone who is very important, say a doctor or family member, do they still have to ask and respect our answer? (Yes).*

Age eight to twelve

- *As your body is changing into an adult's everyone will grow and develop at different rates and in different ways. How does it impact a person's sense of privacy or worth when we comment on how their body is or isn't changing?*
- *Is it ever ok to verbally or physically tease someone about their body or the way they move, talk, dress, and so on? What message does that give someone about their worth as a person? Do you think this hurts them only in the moment or for a long time?*

Age thirteen eighteen

- *Do you think that anyone's actions should mean that another person can touch them without their consent? What if they are acting really sexually or being a tease? Do you think that the concept of being a tease is real or simply a way to blame people who are assaulted? Who benefits from blaming victims versus the perpetrator?*
- *Does respecting someone's body and consent continue if two people are dating or married?*

Privilege and Power

Age seven and under

- *What would make you afraid to say no to someone, either another kid or an adult? Even if they are more popular or older or bigger than you do you still have the right to say no? If you are too afraid or feel intimidated who could you go to for help and support?*
- *If you see someone agreeing to something when they seem afraid how can you support them to speak up for themselves?*

Age eight to twelve

- *If someone agrees to something but they feel like they will be harmed if they say no did they really agree?*
- *Do you think sometimes even people who care about each other pressure each other into things? What can you do to make sure you aren't pressuring or manipulating someone to do what you want?*

Age thirteen to eighteen

- *If someone is in a position of power compared to someone else how would this affect their ability to give and receive honest affirmative consent?*
- *How could someone in power abuse their power to get what they want? Do you think that a relationship with power differences can ever be equal? Why or why not?*

Sexual Agency

Age seven and under

- *Our private parts are private not because we should be embarrassed about them but because they are the most personal and special places on us that belong to only us. So, if someone ever tries to go to those places we must not be afraid to protect them and say "no" and tell someone we trust. Who is someone you could tell, even if you feel embarrassed?*
- *If someone doesn't respect our bodies or minds is that ever our fault? If your friend ever said someone hurt them how could you help your friend? (bystander intervention awareness must begin in elementary school).*

Age eight to twelve

- *As your body grows and changes you will start to feel new physical sensations that feel really good. These are not things to be embarrassed about or feel guilty about enjoying in private by yourself. Do you hear things from your friends about sex feeling good or touching yourself? Does any of it seem confusing or strange? We can talk about that.*
- *What is your favorite part of your body and what is your favorite thing about your personality? If someone says you aren't pretty/handsome or that you are annoying or weird how can you remember the positive things about yourself to block the negative comments from becoming your own beliefs?*

Age thirteen to eighteen

- *What do you think every person is entitled to in a romantic and sexual relationship? Safety, respect, pleasure, and so on.*
- *When people are in their teens they are often told that their feelings, good or bad, aren't as real as an adult's feelings. How do you think this impacts teenagers? Do you think it makes expressing your feelings and believing you will be heard that much harder?*

The above prompts are, of course, simply suggestions to give you ideas for ways to discuss these complex topics with children of any age. Take from them whatever works and then add in your own take on the conversation. Remember the goal is to guide, not to preach, and to listen twice as much as you speak. By having these conversations with your children/students you will glean deep insights into what messages they have already picked up on, what you still need to address, and even new ways of understanding consent and personhood.

THE GIFT OF SHAME-FREE EDUCATION

In writing this book we took time to talk with a number of experts, one of whom is a sex therapist by the name of Dr. Tina Sellers. Dr. Sellers specializes in purity culture myths and how families can merge their concerns for maintaining their personal and religious beliefs with sex positivity.

Sex positivity can exist in every kind of religious and cultural environment and should not be seen as being in conflict with either. As Dr. Sellers shared,

> It's not absence of sex before marriage that is the problem. It has to do with whether or not it is truly the choice of the person or not. I've known plenty of people that have made this decision for themselves and have been perfectly content with it and prepared their sexual selves in all kinds of creative ways for more sexual expansion for later in life. It's about choice.
>
> If a child gets all kinds of sex and gender education in age appropriate ways as they are growing up, and they are able to understand that their body is great, and someone is around to help them learn the nuances of relationships, culture and intimacy, and for whatever reason they decide that they want to keep an aspect of their sexuality on the shelf until later, fine. It is entirely their choice.

The problem lies in toxic concepts of purity. These make women (and all victims) largely responsible for their assailant's actions, make people feel shame about their bodies and desires, all of which can have serious lifelong consequences. Through exploring trauma symptoms that her clients and students were experiencing, Dr. Sellers made a profound discovery:

I was seeing that my students were manifesting signs of sexual assault—their symptoms were exactly the same. I realized I was the first to begin seeing and speaking on what the purity movement and abstinence education had done—it had inadvertently sexually abused an entire generation of youth. It may not have intended to—but the combination of abstinence education which came from the socio-political merging of church and state that happened with the religious right in the early 1980's, and the purity movement of the 1990's had in fact resulted in a fallout of sexual abuse. And now of course, what we are seeing in our current culture is a manifestation of this misogynistic thinking has led in part to the #metoo movement.

When you release youth with this much ignorance and low self-esteem into the world, they are desperately vulnerable to not being able to protect themselves from predatory behavior. They are filled with sexual shame impacting their belief that they have the right to protect themselves. If they question whether they have the right or whether they can protect themselves, they will silence and numb themselves. The vulnerability increases.

Sex education, free from shame, is directly tied to decreasing sexual violence in all forms. It does not require that people engage in sexual activity at a certain time or in a certain way but that they are free to make these personal decisions free from fear and fully informed of all of their options. That is a gift that every young person deserves.

TAKEAWAYS FROM CHAPTER 3

- Personal autonomy is fundamental human right.
- We all have bias and prejudice. By increasing our awareness of these biases, we can work to eradicate them—within ourselves and the world around us.
- Privilege is not a lack of suffering but an ease from suffering caused solely by one's identity.

- By learning and modeling healthy boundaries we can create new normative standards for future generations.
- Sexual agency and sexual subjectivity are critical to creating cultures of consent.
- By imagining the ways that our own upbringing could have been improved we can find avenues for creating impactful change in our children's and student's lives.

NOTES

1. Young-Bruehl, E. (2012). *Childism: Confronting prejudice against children.* Yale University Press.

2. De Zutter, A. W. E. A., Horselenberg, R., & van Koppen, P. J. (2017). The prevalence of false allegations of rape in the United States from 2006–2010. *Journal of Forensic Psychology*, 2, 119.

3. Hanson, R. F., Resnick, H. S., Saunders, B. E., Kilpatrick, D. G., & Best, C. (1999). Factors relating to the reporting of childhood sexual assault. *Child Abuse and Neglect*, (23), 559–569; FBI Law Enforcement Bulletin.

4. Felitti, V. J., Anda, R. F., Nordenberg, D., Williamson, D. F., Spitz, A. M., Edwards, V., & Marks, J. S. (1998). Relationship of childhood abuse and household dysfunction to many of the leading causes of death in adults: The Adverse Childhood Experiences (ACE) Study. *American Journal of Preventive Medicine*, 14(4), 245–258.

5. Geary, C. W., Baumgartner, J. N., Wedderburn, M., Montoya, T., & Catone, J. (2013). Sexual agency and ambivalence in the narratives of first time sexual experiences of adolescent girls in Jamaica: Implications for sex education. *Sex Education*, 13(4), 437–449.

6. Horne, S., & Zimmer-Gembeck, M. J. (2005). Female sexual subjectivity and well-being: Comparing late adolescents with different sexual experiences. *Sexuality Research and Social Policy*, 2(3), 25–40.

7. Dube, S. R., Anda, R. F., Whitfield, C. L., et al. (2005). Long-term consequences of childhood sexual abuse by gender of victim. *American Journal of Preventive Medicine*, 28, 430–438.

Briere, J., & Elliot, D. M. (2003). Prevalence and psychological sequelae of self-reported childhood physical and sexual abuse in a general population sample of men and women. *Child Abuse & Neglect*, 27, 1205–1222.

Holmes, W. C., & Slap, G. B. (1998). Sexual abuse of boys: Definition, prevalence, correlates, sequelae, and management. *Journal of the American Medical Association (JAMA)*, 280, 1855–1862.

Hopper, J. (1998). *Child Sexual Abuse: Statistics, Research, Resources.* Boston, MA: Boston University School of Medicine. *Child Sexual Abuse: A Mental Health Issue.* Kentucky Division of Child Abuse and Domestic Violence.

Wihbey, J. (2015). Global prevalence of child sexual abuse. *Journalist Resource.* (Last on Aug and Updated on 2011 Nov 15). Available from Journ alistsresource.org/studies/./global-prevalence-child-sexual-abuse.

Chapter 4

Decolonizing the Way We Talk about Consent

Cultural Humility and Sexual Scripting

We see the world, not as it is, but as we are—or as we are conditioned to see it.

—Stephen Covey

Many people see these challenging experiences as educators and either give up or become jaded. They blame the students, parents, and the world at large for the ignorance they so easily write off. But what if this isn't exactly ignorance? What if it is something larger? Something we can grow from and with our students on.

Our students are not blank slates, they are not empty vessels, and they do not need us to deposit information into them. We must strive to engage them by promoting questioning and individual reasoning in education.

As Paolo Frier said, "Banking education treats students as objects of assistance; problem posing education makes them critical thinkers." In order to see this fully realized we have to do the work of unlearning everything that had been modeled for us in education. We have to see our students first, understand their truths, earn their trust slowly, and then share how we have used the information we are sharing in our own life and to what benefit. This includes leaving space for disagreement and truths that remained mutually valid even when conflicting.

If we are to teach consent, at any age and in any context, we must be willing to explore the cultural, social, and psychological complexities therein. We must not fill our students with compliance objectives but instead mutually learn and grow in what consent should truly look and feel like.

"We see the world not as it is but as we are." When we see the world as we are we create mythos around "universal experience." We tell ourselves that all of humanity experiences the world as we do. When we travel or interact with communities different than our own we see glimmers of truth in the fallacies of these beliefs. Not everyone eats what we do, thinks as we do, believes what we do, and so on. For some this realization humbles what they previously had upheld as "normal." They will reflect mindfully on the assumptions they have made about universality and realize that while there are common experiences to the human condition, the lens through which we each filter those experiences is as numerous and vast as the stars.

For others, such as our colonializing European ancestors, this will go in the opposite direction. Differences are thus seen as deviations from a "human-neutral" standard. Human neutral meaning white, cisgender, heterosexual, Christian, able-bodied, middle to upper class. Anything different than this is a lesser version of a "normal person" or neutral human.

When speaking across the country about understanding privilege and oppression we have participants do exercises to examine their privileged and marginalized identities. For some, especially young crowds who have heard of these topics before, the exercise is engaging and thought-provoking. But for some, especially older adults with less exposure, the exercise leaves them feeling confused. Their response to even naming their identities is that they don't have any, "I don't really have any" they might say or "I'm just an average/normal person, I'm not privileged or disadvantaged in any real way."

Even though we have just explained what those terms mean and given examples the concept is so foreign to them, colonized ideals and normative standards so ingrained, that cognitive dissonance does not allow the message to sink in yet.

The second interesting response from these participants is to bring up the concept of reverse racism/bias. One might say that being a Christian in the United States means you do not have to fear for your safety or job security by bringing up your faith or wearing a religious symbol such as a cross. In the United States Christianity is seen as the "normal" choice for religion. Be Muslim, Jewish, Sikh, Hindu, and so on and you find yourself having to explain yourself at best and defend your physical and emotional safety at worst.

After saying this some participants will respond by ringing up how they cannot have the ten commandments in schools anymore and that Christianity is under attack. They are used to being in a position of power, a time when Christianity was allowed to be the "human-neutral option." When other religions asked to also post their beliefs they were criticized for forcing their beliefs on others, thus many government buildings had to take a stance of secularism only. Some will say that America was founded as a Christian nation, and so not allowing other religions to have the same kind of access and openness is reasonable.

Yet how often do those same people give money to missionaries who go into Buddhist, Hindu, and Muslim countries trying to convert their citizens to Christianity? Should we not show the same standard to the rest of the world? Sadly, many would say "no," believing that their way of seeing the world is the only right way, continuing the legacy of what colonialism was founded upon.

Here is where the real work of decolonizing begins—within ourselves and our own communities. Even for communities that have been colonized, beliefs about their own lack of worth and savagery are often long internalized. In the concepts of consent and interpersonal violence we see the living generations of communities that were established as LGBTQ-inclusive and matriarchal shaming their communities for being gay, trans, and condemning their women for being sexually empowered.

Colonialism is wiping away the truth of who they are as a people, leaving only the roots of self-hatred and shame in its wake. No one is free from the toxic beliefs that colonialism has left upon our world. Together, through awareness and effort, we can work to heal and challenge this.

A SINGULAR PERSPECTIVE

The majority of sexuality discussions rests upon the tongues of those whose platforms are large and whose words are amplified by privilege and power. In the United States, and many places around the world, our media, textbooks, school curricula, and imagery are narrated and edited by white people, largely men, who are able-bodied, cisgender, heterosexual, middle to upper class, and who have completed the kind of education our community values as academic and worthy of note. This is the same with our conversations around sex and consent. When we talk about sex, whether on the topic of desire or power or pleasure or safety, we are mostly looking at it from a white, financially stable, straight lens.

Now before someone pulls that sentence out of context and goes on a rant about how nobody likes white guys anymore, let me clarify a few essential things for you:

1. There is nothing wrong with white, straight, cisgender men. They are just people, and like every community, they are unique and filled with many wonderful people and a few bad apples with very large mouths who give the rest of them a bad name.
2. Because of a dozen different historical factors, certain communities have gotten a lot of airtime in the media, in the boardroom, in the classroom, and in the bedroom. Because of this fact, it is essential to stop and say, "Hey, who *haven't* we heard from lately (a.k.a. the past thousand years)?"
3. Everyone can grasp privilege once they understand that we all have experienced not being in a position of power. Take, for example, school systems. Most people at some point in primary or secondary school had a not-so-fabulous teacher in their life. Because this person was an adult and in a position of power, they got to hold the mic (literally or figuratively). If they graded you unfairly, made you feel bad, or ignored your need for help, you were at their mercy; that teacher had privilege and power in their role.

Not all teachers who are in those positions of power use it for their own personal gain.

You probably have had or known many teachers who just accepted their privilege and enjoyed parts of it mindlessly and others who want to use it for the utmost good—giving their students more time and care because they have the power to choose to do so in their role. This also means that being a teacher, or anyone in a position of privilege, does not mean you haven't suffered as well.

Many teachers have had students in their class that have made them cry or feel angry. In the end, if brought to a breaking pointing, teachers can leave their job; students can't (easily) leave their school. Teachers and students can feel frustration, but for different reasons. Teachers can say a student isn't respecting their authority; students can say a teacher isn't seeing or hearing them.

Privileged populations suffer, too; they merely aren't suffering because of their identity, and their problems are not being exacerbated by their identity. Anyone can lose their job, but if you are LGBTQ, you can lose your job based solely on who you love or your gender identity. When you start looking for work, anyone can find it hard to find a new position or face rejection, but if you have a nonwhite sounding name, you are likely to be rejected solely because of this factor.

There is nothing wrong with people of privileged status existing, nor are they exempt from unfair life circumstances. The problem is simply the way that social structures and systems value certain lives and experiences more than others.

Take, for example, the arts: we call some art "fine art" and other art "ethnic art" or "ethnic crafts." Why is art from Europe considered to be "fine" and refined but everywhere else on earth considered to be lesser than? Even the term "ethnic" is, in and of itself, a way to create hierarchal terminology that separate "them" from "us."

Who decides who is ethnic? European is an ethnicity, it is only because of colonization that we have been conditioned to think otherwise. Imagine how something that small impacts how our students see themselves? White, straight, cisgender, able-bodied, and so on students think they are normal and students of color, queer, transgender, disabled think that they are separate than the standard instead of everyone being versions of what is common and healthy.

The only reason LGBTQ people have to come out is that everyone is assumed to be straight and cisgender until proven otherwise. If nothing was assumed nothing would have to be announced, or alternatively if nothing was assumed everyone would have to go through the process of deeply considering who they really were and what they truly wanted and then everyone, including straight people, would have to come out and announce what they identify as.

It is with this in mind that we move into the topics of decolonizing consent.

So much of the world—approximately 90 percent[1]—has been colonized by European powers that the histories and experiences of those who were colonized have been silenced, ignored, or erased for generations. In the 1960s and 1970s, many previously colonized countries were exerting their need for independence. Writers such as Robert

Delavignette, John Hargreaves, and David Gardinier started to use a new term to describe the process away from colonization, both socially and politically: thus, the term "decolonization" was born.

For many people new to this discussion, a common rebuttal is, "But that was so long ago, get over it," which is where an understanding of neocolonialism comes in. Neocolonialism is the lived expression of colonialisms roots at work in our current society and beliefs. The reason that we still see that nonwhite names on an application get fewer opportunities, or that there is still so much fear around a non-Christian political leader, is based in both conscious and unconscious bias of who is the "other."

Internally, way back in our primitive brain is a little voice saying, "If they don't look like the people already in power than they can't be trusted." This belief works wonders if you want to take over a country, commit genocide, and leave the scars of your oppression on centuries of people to come, but when we become aware of these facts, we can make a conscious decision to go in a different direction.

DECOLONIZING CONSENT EDUCATION

Until the Lion tells the story, the hunter will always be the hero.

—West African proverb

As we just discussed, history is written by the "winners." What is healthy, safe, natural, and so on is too often a message strong-armed by those whose stories are valued above others. To tell the whole story, we have to step back and expose the narratives of the "lions" who have not yet been given their time to speak and be appreciated.

To decolonize education we must first acknowledge that neither is there a singular lens to see the world nor is there a universal experience, per se. Most of the education we receive in U.S. schools is based on Europe and the United States being the sun in the universe of countries and continents. All other religions, races, languages, and histories are forced to orbit around our importance and truth.

We must realize that different people have different definitions of truth and most of them are based on personal experience. Truth is based on knowing, "I know these truths to be self-evident." Knowing is based on experience and culture and this factor is studied in the field of epistemology. Epistemology looks at how we measure and acquire knowledge. The following are a few examples of epistemological theory:

Foundationalism: There are a few axioms, or statements, from which everything else is true; that is, parallel lines never intersect. Unless they ever do, in which case we need to create a new axiom.
Pragmatism: If it seems true and it works out that is all the proof you need. If every time one prays to my God, my prayers are eventually answered then my God is real. If you pray to my God and nothing ever works out, we will make an excuse such as it wasn't part of God's plan to answer your prayers, but it was part of his plan to answer mine.
Coheritism: Everything is true that doesn't self-contradict. "If I say Europeans are the founders of civilization and I always agree with myself then it is fact." Of course, if someone comes along and says the same of Africa and they always agree with themselves, well then this philosophy doesn't quite work out.

Ontology (the study of reality, existence, and truth) has many fascinating theories and subcategories, including constructivist-ontology. This theory says that our reality and vision of truth comes from the construction of our experiences and exposures. As we grow, we have interactions with the world around us, which confirms or denies our assumptions; this happens from positive feedback, trauma, and formal/informal education. We then approach the rest of life and humanity from this platform: "I know this to be true."

What do we do about the fact that our students have very different epistemological and ontological beliefs? We might say, "Well as research states" or even simply "Our textbook says," and feel that this is justification enough. The reality is that it is not.

Our students' experiences, religions, cultures, identities, and generations bring in diverse and ever evolving truths that will often contract what a book or study says. Every book ever written and every study ever conducted are inherently bias. This doesn't mean they are wrong, but it does mean that they can be correct and another point of view can also be correct and that they can simultaneously contradict each other.

We know this is some very heavy material to digest. But this conversation is so critical and so pivotal to how we approach teaching consent that we cannot continue to ignore it.

Too often we see consent educators, few of whom are actual social scientists, try to make consent something that is cute, quick to explain, and watered down to fit nicely into a meme or YouTube video. Everything is simple if it is watered down or melted to its core, but consent, like any paradigm, is incredibly complex because humanity and the human experience is. The more we address this and discuss it head on with our students the better it will be received and the more applicable it will be. Here are some questions about truth to ask yourself and your students/children:

- What was I taught about consent (explicitly or implicitly)?
- How was consent portrayed in the media I consumed/consume?
- Is it easy to ask for consent and discuss needs/desires/personal boundaries? If not, what culturally holds us back?
- What do we fear about these discussions and negotiations? Name the fear or worst-case scenario.
- Should all cultures require affirmative consent?
- If they should will it look different for different people? What will be the universal common standard? If no, why not?
- Who benefits from consent in a society or relationship?
- How does consent make all interpersonal relationships better? Think consent between parents and child, bosses and employees, politicians and their constituents.

What We Know

Knowledge is limited. You can only live so many places. You can only be assigned so many identities by your community (male, female, nonbinary, black, white, Asian, able-bodied, attractive, unattractive, etc.) or by yourself (straight, gay, trans, progressive, conservative, etc.). We can only be exposed to so much information in our lifetime. Because of this, our version of the truth will always be bias, and our perspective limited. Decolonizing calls on us as educators and parents to think of the ways our students and children see and experience life that may be in conflict with our own view and what we are teaching. This comes up a lot with both consent and sexuality.

The majority of people teaching consent education in this country are white, able-bodied, and politically liberal. A vast number of them are women who work in the social sciences, particularly social work, public health, and education. In and of itself there is nothing wrong with any of this, but it is vital that the people training and speaking on consent and sexuality are formally educated on these topics (more on that later), but it also means that when speaking to a broad audience with a wide range of identities and demographics, the messages can feel homogenized.

Having diverse teachers and presenters benefits children in multiple ways:

1. Seeing a teacher of color has a positive effect on students of all races. For students of color, seeing an example of an educator or advocate who looks like them creates a phenomenon called race-matching (i.e., "*If I can see it, I can be it.*").
2. Recent studies found that all students prefer nonwhite teachers, which is theorized to be because they rarely have teachers of color and enjoy the different perspectives and approaches.[2]
3. Diversity is not limited to race of course. Having teachers of varying gender/sexual identities and expressions, who have had diverse educational experiences, and who have different physical abilities, all go into creating opportunities for students to learn from those unique experiences.

In conversations on sex and relationships, too often we speak from a singular lens. Our work with international students has brought this into perspective for me time and time again. What we think of as common/normal/a given is not the same as someone from Saudi Arabia, Pakistan, Ghana, or Venezuela. Even gender norms are suddenly no longer "norms" if we take a walk around the globe and explore how gender is performed in a mosaic of ways, which we discuss in depth in the next chapter.

Separate from gender differences are the nuances of what we consider appropriate personal boundaries, personal space, or our "bubble." Everyone has a bubble, a sphere of room that we need between ourselves and those around us and culture plays a large role in this. Research published in the *Journal of Cross-Cultural Psychology* looked at the differences in personal space norms around the world.

In Saudi Arabia participants required an average of 3.2 feet between themselves and someone they had a close relationship with, 4.2 feet from a stranger. However, in Argentina for close relationships only 1.3 was requested and 2.5 for strangers.[3] This goes to show how personal needs, feels of respect and safety, are so vast and complex. What personal boundaries and consent look and feel like to one person or one culture will look, feel like, and be communicated differently to someone else.

Teaching students this not only increases cultural humility and inclusion but also helps with dialogue around cross-cultural competencies. If you are dating someone from another part of the world, or even a different part of the same country, you may have very different beliefs about what kind of space and boundaries feel endearing versus threatening.

Add to this that you may have language barriers, even if you are both fluent but one person is communicating in their non-native language, and you have a whole realm of new considerations to discuss in regard to consent.

As Americans, we can see the flaws in our legal and social systems. In our current society there is ongoing uproar over how immigrants at our southern boarder are being treated and mistreated. We can see the imbalances in our justice system and who is profiled and sentenced versus who is let off with a warning.

There are still seven states that force mothers to co-parent with their rapist;[4] there is a mountain of work still to be done in this country on many fronts. In spite of all of this it is essential to remember that these are radical ideas and resources to many people around the world (and backward and antiquated to others). We discussed the school's policy and the laws that protected them but also domestic violence shelters and human resource departments for when they were out and working in American society.

Seeing the reactions on the faces of some of the female students when we explained home domestic violence shelters worked and that going to one would not impact their ability to continue to study in this country was an experience we will never forget. Reminding them that once they graduated and found work the same rights they had at school could be taken up with an HR supervisor was just as important as explaining why we were creating such high standards for consent.

When teaching your international students make sure to bring awareness not only to the overall lesson objective but to the how and why that

American culture has created spaces for these conversations and laws around them. Including the history of laws such as Title IX, labor laws, VAWA, and the laws and statues present (or lacking) in your local area help to inform on how we got to a place to discuss consent in schools and homes.

A very important word of caution here: beware the trap of Western moral superiority. It is far too easy to take the background and current measures of American/Western beliefs about consent, domestic violence, and sexual agency and paint a picture of what "we civilized peoples" do versus the uncivilized rest of the world. Before teaching on these topics do the following exercise, repeat at least once a semester or as you see necessary. Encourage your fellow teachers and staff to do it with you:

- How often do I think of American values being the standard for all of humanity?
- How can I research and learn more about other epistemologies and ways of knowing that are not Western?
- How do my lessons incorporate international perspectives? How about local indigenous perspectives?
- If I am incorporating these perspectives what is the ratio that multi-cultural ethics, norms, and morality are included versus Western? Is the language bias for or against one or the other? What is my tone and pacing when discussing beliefs or knowledge that is different than my own?
- How can I not only incorporate different ideas and schools of thought but give my students platforms to examine and form their own: both as a class and as individuals?
- I will do this by (give examples for each of the above questions).

HOMOGENOUS PERSPECTIVES ON SEX, DATING, CONSENT, AND VICTIMHOOD

There is often a singular image about victims and perpetrators, and this creates a ripple effect on survivors seeking resources. Look at the first page of results on Google Images when you search the term "sexual assault." The images are barely different; they all give the same message about who a victim is and who a perpetrator can be.

Really take a moment to look at the pictures from the search results. What do they all have in common? Is there a pattern? Let us explore the stereotypes of victim and perpetrator in these search results, but also every sexual assault awareness campaign and domestic violence resource ad:

1. *All victims are women.* Yes, women are disproportionately victims of sexual violence compared to men, but they are far from the only ones targeted, though the media would have you believe otherwise. Per the percentage of a population, transgender people are the most likely to be victimized.[5] Men may be less likely to be survivors, but they are also less likely ever to report or be a part of the research, so we don't know the exact numbers. The information we do have tells us that approximately one in six boys is sexually abused by age eighteen,[6] which is a lot. By not showing trans or male survivors we are saying that they don't exist and that the services that are out there aren't for them. The male survivors we have worked with all say they see and feel this and it is harming them immensely.

2. *All the perpetrators are men.* Just like we discussed above, the crime statistics tell us that by and large most victims are women, and most men are the offenders. However, it is tough to see the statistics on how many victims have a female assailant because those cases are so much less often reported or studied. One of the reasons for this is that women who abuse and rape are so often romanticized. Research on female predators shows that they are more likely to use emotional manipulation and blaming the victim for "enjoying it" (especially male victims who neurologically cannot control erections or ejaculation) thus making the victim feel responsible. Family and authorities are also less likely to believe a victim who is reporting a female offender. A lesbian who is saying her partner raped her goes in the face of what most police are trained to believe or deal with in their training.

3. *All of the assaults are violent, and all victims fight back.* One of the most common questions we get from survivors is if they are allowed to call something rape if they didn't say "no" or fight back. The answer is absolutely yes, and that familial and acquaintance rape are the most common sexual assaults in any age

range. Children are most likely to be assaulted by a parent, teens and young adults by friends and romantic partners, and adults by people they know closely, including spouses. When you know and trust someone, you are the most likely to respond by freezing in an assault situation. Your mind is overwhelmed by feeling confused, betrayed, and in denial that this person could hurt you, so it shuts everything down. You won't likely say *anything*, much less no or fight off the person you believed you could trust. By portraying a victim's struggle and vocalization as a requirement to rape, we are silencing millions who need support and are just as harmed and damaged.

4. *All the victims are white.* "Whitewashing" is nothing new, but when it is added to the erasure of sexual assault victims, it has far-reaching effects and long-term impacts. People of color who are abused, assaulted, or go missing are less likely to receive news coverage. Because many resource centers are run and primarily staffed by white people, victims often do not receive culturally humble and applicable services. Sadly, a terrible example of this is how when public figures are accused of crimes, if the accusers are people of color the crimes are rarely investigated until a white victim comes forward. In the case of Bill Cosby's long history of serial rapes, many black women had spoken up and been discredited. It wasn't until a white woman, Andrea Constand, came forward that he was sentenced. This means that violence becomes a culturally accepted fact of life that causes trauma to reverberate for generations.[7]

5. *All victims are gender conforming.* Whether transgender or gender nonconforming (someone whose gender expression does not comply with social expectations) a lack of representation here leads to further marginalization of an already highly vulnerable community. We expect victims to be not only female but also feminine. Masculine-of-center women are often victims of "corrective rape," which attempts to turn them straight (whether they are queer or not). Feminine men also face a great risk of sexual violence for not being masculine enough. To ignore this discussion and faces of victimhood is to ignore reality.

6. *All victims are nondisabled.* Another highly vulnerable and highly ignored population are those with disabilities. Whether the physical

or mental disability is a major factor in victimization, victims with disabilities have often had fewer resources to protect themselves or to seek legal recourse.[8] They are highly vulnerable to manipulation and abuse from caregivers because of their dependency on them. Reporting can be next to impossible because of these compounding factors and yet so little attention is paid to this issue.

Now imagine for a moment that these identities and risk factors are often multiplied in one person. For example,

Women of color victims
Male victims with disabilities
Acquaintance, rapes perpetrated with a female offender

All of these situations can make visibility and access a wall with insurmountable barriers. A large part of decolonizing and creating equitable environments that address the realities of sexual violence and prevention begins with this awareness and accountability. We recently reached out to a respected scholar, Dr. Zelaika Clarke, who studies sexuality and decolonization to gain her perspectives on these topics.

Dr. Zelaika Hepworth Clarke is an anti-colonial and anti-racist sexuality educator, decolonial eroticologist, and clinical sexologist. They cofounded a sexuality studies concentration program at Goddard College in Vermont that focuses on social justice and decolonial perspectives. As she points out, decolonizing sexuality and consent means looking at historical and institutionalized trauma,

Being aware of the past and risks involved while navigating toxic patriarchal power structures can provide insight into the present and hopefully offer examples of baselines from which to grow, overcome or eliminate in order to create a different reality or context to thrive in.

Historical perspectives of atrocities in the past might be informative in contextualizing current events and factors that contribute to rape culture. We must also make room to conceptualize what a culture without rape would be like so as to not perpetuate the conditions that created and fostered rape culture.

While culturally specific sexual violence prevention strategies might not be universally effective. Awareness of how the system is problematic and past issues within the law or institutions is a good step to take.

TAKEAWAYS FROM CHAPTER 4

- Everything, including this book, is biased.
- We are all limited in how we see the world because we filter it through our experiences and the beliefs formed there within.
- Privilege does not mean freedom from hardship. It means that particular hardships were not directly caused by a certain identity.
- To holistically address consent education we must discuss decolonizing both consent and educational systems.
- Society has conditioned us to see victimhood through a very singular lens. Victims (as well as perpetrators) come in all shapes, sizes, ages, gender, and identities.
- We must be mindful of our explicit and implicit bias in doing this work in order to serve all children/students effectively.

NOTES

1. Laycock, S. (2012). *All the Countries: And the Few We Never Got Round To*. The History Press.

2. Cherng, H.-Y. S., & Halpin, P. F. (2016). The importance of minority teachers: Student perceptions of minority versus white teachers. *Educational Researcher*, *45*(7), 407–420.

3. Sorokowska, A., Sorokowski, P., Hilpert, P., Cantarero, K., Frackowiak, T., Ahmadi, K., & Pierce, J. D. (2017). Preferred interpersonal distances: A global comparison. *Journal of Cross-Cultural Psychology*, *48*(4), 577–592.

4. Where rapists can gain parental rights, By Breeanna Hare and Lisa Rose, CNN Updated 1:06 PM ET, Thu November 17, 2016

5. FORGE, 2005, Sexual Violence in the Transgender Community Survey, unpublished data; Kenagy, G. (2005). The health and social service needs of transgender people in Philadelphia. *International Journal of Transgenderism*, *8*(2/3), 49–56; Kenagy, G., & Bostwick, W. (2005). Health and social service needs of transgendered people in Chicago. *International Journal of Transgenderism*, *8*(2/3), 57–66.

6. Briere & Elliot, Prevalence and psychological sequelae, 1205–1222.
Finkelhor, D., Hotaling, G., Lewis, I. A., & Smith, C. (1990). Sexual abuse in a national survey of adult men and women: Prevalence, characteristics, and risk factors. *Child Abuse & Neglect*, *14*, 19–28.

7. Donovan, R. A. (2007). To blame or not to blame: Influences of target race and observer sex on rape blame attribution. *Journal of Interpersonal Violence*, *22*(6), 722–736.

Weist et al., Sexual assault in Maryland: The African American experience, 2007.

8. Keilty, J., & Connelly, G. (2001). Making a statement: An exploratory study of barriers facing women with an intellectual disability when making a statement about sexual assault to police. *Disability & Society, 16*(2), 273–291.

Casteel, C., Martin, S. L., Smith, J. B., Gurka, K. K., & Kupper, L. L. (2008). National study of physical and sexual assault among women with disabilities. *Injury Prevention, 14*(2), 87–90.

Chang, J. C., Martin, S. L., Moracco, K. E., Dulli, L., Scandlin, D., Loucks-Sorrel, M. B., . . . & Bou-Saada, I. (2003). Helping women with disabilities and domestic violence: Strategies, limitations, and challenges of domestic violence programs and services. *Journal of Women's Health, 12*(7), 699–708.

Chapter 5

Teaching Consent
Curriculum Design and Diffusion

Over the past few chapters we have built a solid foundation for what consent is, why it is essential, and many of the sociopsychological factors that go into this topic. By now you hopefully feel energized and intrigued to start or expand your consent education and modeling for your students, children, and community.

You should also have established an understanding that there is not a "one-and-done" conversation but more of an ongoing and progressively building dialogue that must begin in home and be continued in schools. This can seem like an impossible task that feels both inspiring and insurmountable.

No one knows this better than those of us who have dedicated our lives to doing this work. No matter how passionately we love the mission, no matter how much we would never trade this job or our calling for anything, this is still a brutal, unappreciated, and exhausting work.

Have you ever heard the adage "How do you eat an elephant? One bite at a time?" Consent culture is very much an elephant, maybe a whole heard! Only by strategically approaching our goals and objectives we can eat it all, piece by piece. In this chapter, I want to look more closely at how this works in a school setting.

The school environment is designed with one ultimate purpose in mind—learning. Even though that often takes many forms and comes with its own loaded debate over the ideal way to accomplish this, learning is always the goal none the less. Learning is not rote memorization or passing a test, and it is not state standards and formative scores; learning is evolution, learning is an enhancement on who we are into who we can become, and learning is personal.

What we learn can never be taken from us; it is woven into the fabric of our soul. We become what we learn, and it becomes part of us. We then teach it, whether formally or unconsciously, and it becomes part of another.

This is the power of education.

Because of the standardized testing and the way that many teachers are judged and graded themselves there are lots of reasons that they may ignore a teachable moment when a student brings up a real-world topic in class. I think this is one of the greatest losses to the educational experience of our time.

We spend so much time with these young minds, and not only are we the teachers, but our students are the teachers of each other as well. There are a few things as beautiful as a fellow child or teen assisting and enlightening their peer.

What better to impart in our learning environments than values? If we want our children to walk away with anything from an educational environment, it is a better understanding of themselves and those around them. We know some will snicker and say that school is about teaching skills that prepare you for a career and the workforce, not touchy-feely stuff, but it is essential to clarify that one is directly connected to the other.

EMOTIONAL QUOTA

Of all of the seminars we get asked to present on, one of the most popular for international business continuing education is on emotional intelligence. The focus on hard skills is becoming a thing of times gone by. In the present and future job market interpersonal skills, or soft skills as they are referred to, are the resume builders of the future.

Schools need to prepare students for college and careers of the future, which means understanding how to work with diverse groups, how to respect boundaries and read comfort levels, and when to move forward versus hold back. All of these are directly connected to affirmative consent.

WHAT ABOUT THE BOYS?

One of the most interesting comments we hear from parents of sons is that they want more of the focus to be on helping their sons not get in trouble for sexual assault or harassment. They feel confused by how our culture has defined boundaries in the #MeToo era and want to have the conversations that will help their boys respect boundaries, or at least not get in a situation they could be in trouble for.

Sadly, the latter seems to be the main focus—as many of these parents still believe that most of these allegations are false reports. False reporting is incredibly rare. For adults the rate of false reporting is approximately 5 percent[1] and for children it goes down to 1 percent.[2]

Instead, the focus must shift from "not getting our sons in sticky situations" to helping everyone communicate, read, and respect boundaries. Second, we must prepare them for how to speak to interact with members of all sexes in a way that honors the dignity of each life, including their own.

This means going through puberty, college, and beginning their career with a clear and comprehensive understanding of what violates another's agency and personhood. Here are some conversations to have with your sons. These are all things we have been or will be discussing with our own sons. Adjust them for each child's age and ability and feel free to include your own experiences and the experiences of people you trust and who can add value to the conversation.

Conversations for Our Sons

- *What are some differences you see in how boys, girls, and nonbinary kids are treated?*
- *What are some things people let boys do or get away with that girls are criticized for? What about things girls can do or feel that boys are told not to?*
- *What does treating boys and girls, men and women, differently do to them? How do you think this affects nonbinary or trans kids and adults?*
- *What would the world look like if there was only healthy expression of gender, not toxic ones? What makes femininity or masculinity toxic versus healthy anyway?*

- *How do you think boys and men contribute to rape culture? How are they impacted by it?*
- *Do you think boys and men are hypersexualized in rape culture narratives? Like all boys/men want all sex or should be grateful for it?*
- *How do you see male sexual assault portrayed in the media? Is it still a punch line for a joke? Do male victims get the support they deserve? What would that look like?*
- *What should you say if your friend says that they have been bullied/ harassed/assaulted? If the friend is a girl, what if your friend is a boy, trans or nonbinary?*
- *Who benefits from consent? (Everyone).*
- *If honest, open, and safe communication was normalized how would this help young men, women, and nonbinary teens and adults?*

As psychologist and male victim expert, Dr. David Lisak, told me, "What boys need to hear and to learn is no different than what girls need to hear and learn. And while girls are less likely to perpetrate sexual violence, rates of female perpetration are not zero. So girls too need to learn about affirmative consent and respect for boundaries." The messages we tell our sons about their rights and responsibilities should look no different that the messages we convey to girls.

HOW ARE VALUES LEARNED?

As children and teens, we are sponges for values, morals, and ethics. As our brain develops in the first twenty-five years of life, we are continually observing, receiving input, and pruning our values tree. We watch what works for others, listen to what they say, and weigh it against our trial-and-error data. During the first three to five years of life, we define what love is.

We observe how our primary caregivers treat us and subconsciously form a permanent idea of how it feels and looks to be loved. If our caregivers show us grace, kindness, and consistency, we will forever seek that in loving connections. If we are ignored, manipulated, or abused we will also seek that out and believe it shows that the person loves us.

For many, this appears to be bad news, a life sentence to painful relationships and heartbreak; but it is not. It is merely a wake-up call, an invitation to awareness, and an alarm to alert us to what we are imprinting on the next generation. Our ideas and connections about love, morality, and consent can all be formed and reformed—we have to be aware and make the right choices in the information we digest and the patterns we perpetuate.

Values can be taught, and consent is a value. Rape-acceptance beliefs are one of the ways we can tangibly research and measure how an individual or community sees sexual violence and consent. We can look at this by examining what myths they see as truthful, that is, blaming victims for assaults, believing that men cannot control their aggression, thinking that trans women are tricking their partners and thus bring an assault on themselves.

Research can be subjective and manipulated. Therefore, we do have to look at each study critically and have it examined and confirmed by a group of scholar peers. But research is still an invaluable tool to measure behaviors, modify practices, and formulate best practices. In this chapter, we will look at what research tells us about how values can be taught, the best way to teach consent values, and how to implement this education across the curriculum and in partnership with parents.

Values and moral education have been taught since the beginning of human society. Every community, every tribe, every nation, religion, and philosophy must teach what they see as right and wrong. They must teach this in a way that will make their young grow and develop to want to conform to these ideals. While some may say that values and morals should only be taught at home, we must remember that humanity has never learned solely in a nuclear family or "home" as we define it today.

Humans are communal and have for almost all of our history existed and learned in tribes or groups of family units. This benefits the young as they learn from different teachers, with different experiences, and different ages of development. This allows the child to understand how, even with asynchronous view on morality, each person will interpret and relay this in a unique way. In the modern era schools have become an excellent opportunity to educate and discuss these topics.

The concern, of course, becomes, in a multifaceted society, who decides morality? The answer lies in teaching these challenging topics from a cognitive-developmental approach (CDA) with a Socratic delivery.

One of the founders of CDA and values education was John Dewey. Dewey was an American philosopher, teacher, and psychologist who wrote some of the most foundational theories in progressive education to date. On moral education he stated the following:

> *The aim of education is growth or development, both intellectual and moral. Ethical and psychological principles can aid the school in the greatest of all constructions—the building of a free and powerful character. Only knowledge of the order and connection of the stages in psychological development can insure this* (Emphasis is mine).

Dewey was largely influenced by Kohlberg's and Paiget's theories on cognitive development and moral education, yet he still remains uniquely structured from his predecessors. The following are Dewey's three stages of development:[3]

1) *Premoral or pre-conventional level*: This stage is most common throughout the elementary school years though some people do not progress past it ever. This stage is dominated by rules and obedience. A stage one person does what they are told because they were told to; there is no other motivation to obey but to not get in trouble and to conform.
2) *Conventional level of behavior*: The conventional stage is where the majority of children, teens, and adults move to but also remain. Seeking approval, conformity, and popularity are all part of this second stage. The majority of people do what they do to remain in good standing with their community. They do what is seen as right or good because they want to please those around and above them.
3) Autonomous level of behavior: Rarely achieved but often admired autonomous behavior means doing what is right because it is what the individual truly feels is best for others, the community, and humanity. No matter what is seen as normal or acceptable this person will do what they sincerely believe is right even if that means ostracization.

The CDA to education is one of the three main theories on moral teaching. Everyone has been subjected to one of the three, each having their pros and cons, and each producing similar yet uniquely differentiated results. The other two schools of moral education are as follows:

Indoctrination Education

The military, Boy Scouts, and churches have all long held dear to the indoctrination method of moral education (often called character education or character development lessons). Indoctrination theory believes that values and virtues are steadfast and that certain select character qualities should be epitomized.

For example, the Boy Scouts choose trustworthy, loyal, helpful, friendly, courteous, kind, obedient, cheerful, thrifty, brave, clean, and reverent. On the other hand, the national organization 4H selected clearer thinking, higher loyalty, service, and better living. The U.S. Army has chosen loyalty, duty, respect, selfless service, honor, integrity, and personal courage. Each of the groups choose to utilize the indoctrination method which requires self-selecting a different set of core values, which often change over time.

These values are preached vehemently and held as the pinnacle standard for being a moral and upstanding member of the group. This method discourages questioning or dialogue as to keep the purity of the standards it is promoting. The problem is each educator or instructor will interpret and communicate these beliefs differently affecting the uniformity of the messages and diluting the standard. Indoctrination is often unpleasant and confusing for new members and recruits and can create a climate of fear, and its belief that certain values are universal is an ever-eroding framework in an evermore globalized society.

Values Clarification (VC)

Because of the harshness and inflexibility of indoctrination values education, a second theory was developed. Values clarification (VC) theory promotes Socratic dialogue between educators and students that elicits a personal response from each person individually. Students are engaged in order to rationally understand what values exist, what different views on morality are, and what rings true for them as autonomous beings.

It then goes to reason that no two students will walk away from VC the same, leaving this theory in the family of modern moral relativity schools of thought. Taken to an extreme, this is where some can argue that nothing is genuinely wrong if the individual acting believes they are right.

The third model, the CDA, blends elements of the first two and creates a rational, Socratic, but well-defined middle path. CDAs can be understood as such:

In addition to having more definite aims than values clarification, the moral development approach restricts value education to that which is moral or, more specifically, to justice. This is for two reasons. First, it is not clear that the whole realm of personal, political, and religious values is a realm which is nonrelative, i.e., in which there are universals and a direction of development. Second, it is not clear that the public school has a right or mandate to develop values in general.

In our view, value education in the public schools should be restricted to that which the school has the right and mandate to develop: an awareness of justice, or of the rights of others in our Constitutional system. While the Bill of Rights prohibits the teaching of religious beliefs, or of specific value systems, it does not prohibit the teaching of the awareness of rights and principles of justice fundamental to the Constitution itself. When moral education is recognized as centered in justice and differentiated from value education or affective education, it becomes apparent that moral and civic education are much the same thing. This equation, taken for granted by the classic philosophers of education from Plato and Aristotle to Dewey, is basic to our claim that a concern for moral education is central to the educational objectives of social studies[4] (Emphasis is mine).

When teaching consent to young people, or people of any age for that matter, it is important to not let our passion create an indoctrination framework. We see so many advocate educators who seek to impart how deeply they care about getting their message across that they end up alienating their audience. On the flipside we see indoctrination coming from the compliance world.

Compliance in and of itself requires a solid dosage of fear—do this or *else*—which is the core of indoctrination moral theory. This mindset often comes from those fearful of liability above all (lawyers and HR managers need to be mindful of this). People who promote compliance-focused models think that if the consequences are harsh enough then no one will dare cross the line and disobey. Instead this breeds a contempt for both the institution and the message.

Because all theories are on a spectrum and human nature often causes the pendulum to swing there is also a danger in leaning toward a VC model when talking about consent and sexual violence. In desiring to move away from a legalistic mindset we can find a situation where setting clear guidelines and principles is shunned and everything is debatable.

For those of us trained to question and turn every argument over and over (academics and activists, that can be us), there comes a time when we let what ifs to take precedent and all borders to dissolve in an attempt to be radically inclusive and intellectual. The problem here is anything can be argued for, even rape and abuse, thus defeating our entire purpose of educating and informing.

In the end consent education must have parameters that are designed with the objective in mind. If we want a world where interpersonal violence is not tolerated in any form then we must be clear on what that constitutes. At the same time, within those objectives, we must give room for discussion and debate. Our students are relying on us to be guides on their exploration of what personal autonomy and mutually respectful relationships are, but not to tell them the answers as absolutes. In find their own definitions and examples they begin to take full ownership over the more overarching concept of consent.

In doing so we, as the educators and experts, are exposed to new layers and understandings of the topic ourselves.

CROSS-CURRICULAR DESIGN

Nothing done well, thought out intentionally, or executed effectively is ever done in haste. The same is true when we are teaching values, and in particular, values that carry such weight and that will be essential to personal and professional success as the concepts and virtue of affirmative consent. Have you ever thought of consent as a valuable moral or virtue before? If not, we would strongly encourage you to stop for a moment and think of it in that way. Throughout this book, we have examined the sociocultural and communal aspects of affirmative consent.

You may have opened this book thinking this was a conversation about health education, sex education, or social propriety. We hope that you are now at a point where you understand that what we are talking about is a complete and total unlearning, overturning, and reimagining of all interpersonal communication and contact.

This is no small aim, but it is also not an impossible line, not by any means. What it requires is the dedication and patience of individuals and communities. As we also discussed one of the perfect places for this to begin and to be nurtured is in the classroom.

Often, people think consent education is only about sex, and it certainly is extremely important in sexual contacts. But consent is so much more than something that is intertwined with the mechanics of sexual intercourse or even romantic relationships. Consent has to do with everything from how we communicate with each other, how we approach one another, to how we share our most intimate and vulnerable parts of ourselves.

Because of this, and because of the depth and breadth of what we are trying to teach and learn, there is no one singular class, primary age, or singular moment when this conversation should happen. Consent education has to be lifelong and cross-curricular.

Now that more and more schools are starting to see the importance of cross-curricular implementation and design for almost any subject this is a wonderful opportunity to bring together cross-curricular pedagogy with affirmative consent legislation in education. Consent is not something that she should only be taught in eighth-grade health class.

It is undoubtedly not something that should only be taught during orientation and through an online course during your freshman year of college, which is what is currently the case all across America. As an educator I have personally taught consent, healthy boundaries, and human rights in English classes, health classes, and social studies courses. It also belongs in science, math, and as an overall separate conversation that is woven within each subject matter.

It is understandable that this might be hard for many to imagine and comprehend. How on earth are you going to put consent education in a mathematics course? Simple, it can be added into the subject of statistics to explore the prevalence of these issues and statistical misconceptions. What about science? Science is a wonderful place to explore chemical reactions that go on in the body and mind during decision-making and trauma. If students are studying biology, we should also be integrating it with psychology. Second, science has a fascinating history with consent in regard to research and experiments as well as ethical boundaries.

In English, we can read research and explore different perspectives on this topic. Having a platform where students have to write about their feelings, views, and experiences with consent is an excellent way to promote reading and writing and to solidify the values that we are seeking clarification on.

Even in something like physical education consent can be modeled. Physical education often involves a lot of physical contact with other people being aware of personal boundaries and encouraging respectful contact and seeking consent before touching someone is an area that athletics certainly has room to grow.

We see a lot of sexual misconduct cases coming from high school and college athletic departments. There is still culture that promotes toxic gender stereotypes and expectations and monks those two expressed in cells outside of the gender binary which can become a petri dish for abuse and violence.

It is because consent is part of every single field because every single field has to do with interpersonal interaction, that this curriculum has to be spread and planted in all of these courses. It is a fantastic opportunity for educators to work together across grade levels, making sure that each year students are introduced to another piece of this dialogue, and across subject matter making consent in the multidimensional and holistic learning experience.

The following is an example of what starting a consent education curriculum could look like in a K–12 setting as a topic that is covered in elementary, middle, and high school. Many parts will need to be repeated and developed each year in order for the messages to stick and become normalized: just remember how many times you learned fractions or about the Civil War in your K–12 years. Teaching consent over and over is certainly no less important.

Step 1: Teach the Faculty and Staff First. Get everyone on the same page and messaging around the new consent education infusion as well as everyone's responsibilities around Title IX response and reporting.

Step 2: Educate the Parents. Talk to the parents first, before the kids. This gives them tools for addressing these topics at home as well as creating a safe space to explore their concerns and help them understand their student's rights.

Step 3: Plant the Curriculum. Think of consent education as wild flowers—growing all over your school and popping up in unexpected places. Just as sex should not be a singular solemn talk neither should consent. Here are some topics to talk about per age group:

Elementary

Bodily Autonomy—Each person's rights to feel safe and comfortable in their body

Boundaries—Understanding our unique needs for physical and emotional space

Understanding What We Need to Feel Safe—Discussions of physical and emotional safety

Active Listening—How to listen to really hear what each person is saying and disagreeing without conflict

Gender Diversity—What gender is, isn't, and how to appreciate gender differences and identities

Cultural Inclusiveness—Understanding gender, boundaries, and the way that our cultures influence our needs and beliefs about these topics

Diverse Families—Exploring how families include different members with unique gender, age, and cultural identities.

What to Do If Someone Hurts You or Your Friend—How to support a friend who is being abused, who to tell, how to make sure they feel believed and safe.

Middle School

Anatomy and Physiology/Body Diversity—An expansion on body diversity including colorism, fat/skinny shaming, the true meaning of health (outside of colonized norms), and how pubescent changes and adult bodies are varying and unique

Gender Around the World and Throughout History—Gender through a historical, cross-cultural, and neuro-inclusive lens

Healthy Relationships—Understanding what constitutes a healthy relationship. Relationships that include romantic, platonic, and familial connections. Understanding abusive dynamics and how the media/society normalizes toxic tropes

Bystander Intervention—How to effectively and safely intervene when someone is in potential danger or discloses abuse.

Emotional Intelligence—What emotional intelligence is, empathy in action, and how soft skills help you in all areas of life

High School

Rape Culture—Defining rape culture, rape-acceptance beliefs, and what a culture that normalizes consent looks and feels like

Affirmative Consent—What consent requires; from affirmation to enthusiasm, to safety

Dating/Domestic Violence—What toxic, abusive, and unhealthy relationships include. What to do if you or someone you know is in one

Healthy Relationships—Creating the relationships you want, not settling, knowing your needs, and communicating what you want effectively

Conflict Resolution—Dealing with conflict in all relations from work to a partnership

Sexual Agency/Subjectivity—Knowing your rights to safe and pleasurable sexual experiences. Overcoming sexual shame and creating mutually respectful and pleasurable experiences.

BUILDING BRIDGES WITH PARENTS AND SCHOOLS

There are few relationships as caustic and as connected as that of parents and educators. Both love children, want the best for them, but feel at times threatened or uncomfortable with the other. In working in consent education, you are likely to come across schools, teachers, or parents (or all three) who do not see eye to eye on this topic.

The most common reaction is to avoid the subject altogether, bury your head in the sand, and hope that someone braver than you pushes it forward. Please, do not do this. It will benefit no one in the long or short term to avoid these uncomfortable conversations. Instead, you must arm yourself, whether you are a parent or educator, with the whys. Why is this important? Why now? Connected to the whys is the hows. How will the effectiveness of this be measured? How will this be taught?

Remember too that for the adults in every category many of these conversations are new to them as well and present feelings of cognitive dissonance as well as defensiveness. No one wants to see themselves or their generational/cultural beliefs as problematic. To overcome this, we have to build bridges of understanding. Start your consent education program by educating teachers and administrators and then parents and interested community members. Make sure that your facilitators are subject matter experts who are comfortable with fielding confrontational questions and redirecting divisive crowds.

Parents and educators must work together in order for consent education to be lasting and effective. Will this be accomplished easily and quickly, probably not. But nothing worthwhile ever is. If we remain focused, welcome feedback/evolution, and see the challenges ahead as mountains we have yet to climb, then we can reach the valleys we hunger for. By working to help everyone learn and come onboard, and create schools, communities, and households that value consent. We can be the changes we want to see in our world.

TAKEAWAYS FROM CHAPTER 5

- Consent education is really about teaching morals, values, and life skills.
- Teaching consent prepares students to comply not only with student conduct and create safe learning environment but also emotional intelligence for the workplace and adult world.
- By understanding how children and teens learn values, we can create consent education that is impactful and long-lasting.
- Consent must be more than an isolated conversation. It needs to be infused into every subject area.
- Consent can be taught, age-appropriately at every age and to every audience.

NOTES

1. De Zutter et al., The prevalence of false allegations of rape in the United States from 2006–2010.
2. Hanson et al., Factors relating to the reporting of childhood sexual assault.
3. Ord, Jon. (2012). John Dewey and experiential learning: Developing the theory of youth work. *Journal of Youth & Policy, 108.*
4. Kohlberg, L. (1975). The cognitive-developmental approach to moral education. *The Phi Delta Kappan, 56*(10), 670–677.

Chapter 6

Breaking Down the Binary
Gender-Responsive Frameworks

THE PARADOX OF GENDER

Every cartoon, fairy tale, movie, and story we hear has hints of toxic expressions of gender in them. Our relatives and friends may grant us the courtesy of a smile and nod when we tell them we want to raise our children gender-neutral but still purchase onesies with "Princess" and "Lady Killer" on it. Gender, in its worst form, is something that still pervades almost all aspects of our daily lives.

This can be immediately bubble bursting and disheartening; we want what we believe is best for our children so then why is the world fighting us on our enlightenment? The answer is simple because change is hard. It is far easier, and sometimes more pleasant, to continue on the path we are on. Even if there is a better way, most human beings will reject new information in favor of the way things have been. The idea being better to live with the not-so-great option than do the work of evolving toward something better.

We are mammals who love habit and gender roles is a deeply held habit and belief. Be patient with yourself and others—this is a journey that requires examining, uncovering, unlearning, and then relearning how we see ourselves and much of our world. This won't happen overnight, but it can occur over time: and that is a change worth waiting for.

After finding out one is pregnant the second piece of information millions of modern-day parents all over the world want to know is if they are expecting a boy or a girl. Pink or Blue, Ruffles or Riffles, Bows or

Bowties, Touchdowns or Tutus, Tractors or Tiaras, Staches or Lashes, Guns or Glitter; these are a sampling of catchy questions posed on gender reveal cakes and banners. While well-intended they leave little to the imagination as to how deeply ingrained gender roles and dichotomies are even to this day.

Gender reveals parties reveal so much more than the chromosomes or genitals of a fetus; they uncover our culture's obsession with child ownership and forcing young humans into tiny boxes of predetermined cultural expectations. Research has shown that because we can now know the sex (we cannot tell the gender expression or identity yet) of a baby in utero, parents begin treating their children differently before they even take their first breath.

As infants, babies, and toddlers are often described as being more emotional or sensitive, whereas boys are easily described as tough and strong, even though little evidence exists that these are innate traits. We do see differences in brain scans of boys and girls, but every variation can be contributed to how the child perceives themselves in their gender role and expectations on its performance.

Tell a baby its job is to grow to be sweet and gentle, and those parts of the brain will expand, tell it to be smart and aggressive, and those regions will be nourished as well. We do not come into being with these traits because of our chromosomes but because of how our community directs out malleable brains to develop. Our relationship and parenting responsibility begin long before our babies are placed in our arms.

GENDER: FOR BETTER OR WORSE

To ever embrace a different view on gender we must understand what it is and how it can negatively affect us. We are programmed to ask, "What's in this for me?" How will we personally see a benefit within myself, my community, and my children by relearning gender norms?

First of all, what is gender? Gender is the way in which we assign roles, expectations, and duties to individuals in our society based on their genitalia. The doctor, midwife, or parent looks between the baby's legs, sees what they decide is a penis or vagina (more on this in the intersex section), and proudly proclaim the child's gender and sex. Sex is based on the belief that chromosomes—ideally a nice clear XX for a girl or an XY for a boy—can define gender.

Those chromosomes then cause primary (genitals and sex organs) and secondary (breasts, hair, muscle tone) sexual characteristics to develop in a person. Just because a person has primary and secondary sex characteristics does not mean that our mental understanding, personal expression, or individual identity align with the gender norms connected to our sex. Sex is biological and physiological; gender is social, cultural, and personal. Even the idea of XX and XY being assigned to gender and sex classification is new—something that was debated over and decided between the 1920s and 1950s.[1] Below are a few of the standard terms and expressions assigned to each gender in the binary system.

Please don't read them and say, "Oh I know men and women who aren't like these stereotypes." Yes, we have progressed past many places of rigidity but we still exist in a world where femininity is devalued, children are forced to abide by strict gender standards or are bullied, and where adults who do not strictly conform to their gender or the binary system are at a considerable risk or abuse, assault, and homicide. This is still very much our reality in American, and much of the world, today.

Girl/Woman

Pronouns: She/Her/Hers.
Dress: dresses, skirts, blouses, V-neck T-shirts, heels, pumps, ballet flats, fitted jeans, panties, bras, purses, makeup.
Hair: long, soft, brushed, relaxed, frames face.
Colors: pink, coral, yellow, purple, pastels, white.
Voice: soft, musical, lilting, gentle, approachable, not demanding.
Walk: shifts hips side to side, sort strides, walks on balls of feet, little sound.
Hand/arm movement: active with hand expressions, soft handshake, offers hand palm down, examines hands palm down, lets hands rest together or near the face, elbows close to the body.
Sitting: ankles crossed, knees close together, shoulders in.
Standing: shifts weight to one leg, head slightly down eyes upward, arms by the side or clasped.

Sexual desires: desires penetration, desires to please partner, excited by masculinity, orgasms quickly and more than once.

Adjectives: Positive—pretty, sweet, kind, maternal, nurturing, helpful, submissive, pleasant, agreeable. Negative—plane, fat, slut, whore, nympho, needy, emotional, cold, nagging, sensitive, irrational, talkative, bossy.

Boys/Men

Pronouns: He/Him/His.

Dress: pants, crew neck T-shirts, button downs, ties, flat shoes, wallet, baseball caps, fedoras, suites, tuxedos.

Hair: short, if longer not overly kept, natural colors.

Colors: blue, black, brown, gray, dark colors, no glitter or sparkle

Voice: deep, steady, gruff

Walk: even and wide stride, hips square to ground, walks on heels of feet, heavy steps.

Hand/arm movement: arms swing when walking, elbows out, hands rest on legs or are crossed.

Sitting: legs spread, feet grounded, back straight.

Standing: tall spine, arms folded, feet carry weight evenly.

Sexual desires: desires to penetrate but never be penetrated, aggressive/dominant, hopes partner is enjoying it, takes a while to climax (can make it last all night).

Adjectives: Positive—powerful, strong, protective, self-assured, smart, wise, handsome, assertive, level-headed, ladies' man. Negative—entitled, chauvinistic, callous, unfeeling, predatory.

Sit with these lists for a minute. Add to it in your mind and reflect on how these norms and expectations have impacted you and the way you interact with the other gender. What assumptions do you make based on gender roles? Do you ever feel repulsed when you see someone behaving in a way that contradicts these? What is it is an extreme stretch across the binary such as a man wearing makeup and not as a joke—Would you ridicule them even privately? What about women who wear a buzz cut or get married in a suit—Are they less of a woman to you? We cannot move into a world that embraces consent without examining gender and how gender roles in a toxic form are a cornerstone of rape culture and rape-acceptance beliefs.

It is essential to clarify that gender itself is not inherently toxic. Just as religion, politics, or any other social construct can be positive or neutral when done mindfully and with balance—all can be healthy ways of identifying and expressing our beliefs.

It is only when something is all or nothing, where it complies with a strict standard or is harmed, and where there is no room for growth or difference that something becomes toxic. Gender is the same.

Recent discussions on Toxic Masculinity (TM) have led certain social and political commentators to reply that "men and masculinity are under attack." What they are completely ignoring is that concerns about toxic extremes of masculinity are neither natural, healthy, nor innate. TM, or femininity for that matter, is entirely separate from healthy gender expression and identity.

Gender can be a beautiful part of understanding ourselves and the world around us, it is only when we excuse toxic behaviors (not being able to express a full range of emotions, not being emotionally intelligent, not taking on a balance in work and family life) as part of our gender or limit what people can feel, enjoy, or experience because of their chromosomes that we cross a line that can be, and should be, examined and redirected.

Gender stereotypes are not neutral; they have measurable and lasting impacts. These effects can be observed in everything from the kind of medical care we receive to our academic performance. In multiple studies done on gender and testing simply telling the participants that test would measure gender differences drastically impacted how women scored. Similarly, when men are reminded of this factor they scored significantly better.[2] Thinking about our gender, and the stereotypes of it, make us change the way we function for better and worse.

Even when explaining health concerns women face additional barriers to men. Women's expressions of pain are often brushed off as whining, complaining, excused as low pain tolerance. Therefore, female patients must perform in a way, that is, "not to appear too strong or too weak, too healthy or too sick, or too smart or too disarranged" in order to be deemed credible patients.[3] This creates an incredible extra toll on the patients in the form of emotional labor and anxiety, something which male patients have not been shown to have to deal with.

Emotional labor is not the only extra work that women take on. They also take on additional physical labor. Whether working inside or outside the home women have to work additional hours of manual labor called the second shift. Second shift work has been documented and theorized since the 1980s and comes under scrutiny as social commenters try and say that this home and family labor gap is allegedly closing.[4]

The reality is it very much still exists.[5] When a child is sick at school most often the mother is called first, mothers are consistently asked where their children are when they are at work, and even being a mother is still seen as something all women deep down desire and long for.

For men TM impacts boys' and men's mental and physical health. Men are less likely to seek mental health treatment, even in extremely stressful situations.[6] This is lack of support. Men are impacted by all of the stressors of daily life as well as incidents of trauma; they need mental health care as much as women and girls who are more often encouraged to get professional help and resources. Even in regard to social media use and exposure, TM is connected to overuse and depression.[7]

Thinking about our gender, and the stereotypes that go along with it, can have an impact on how we function. This is called stereotype threat, or the study of how stereotypes have negative repercussions on the people they box in and demean.

For example, female students who take exams in math or sciences, and who are reminded of their gender before taking the exam, perform worse than if they take a similar exam with no reminder of their gender.[8] We become what is expected of us, defeating ourselves before we even try, even though this is completely subconscious.

Think of how stereotypes impact both victims and aggressors in sexual violence situations. A female victim blames herself for not fighting off her abuser or convinces herself she gave mixed messages and was at fault. A male victim thinks that because he had an erection while being assaulted that he must have deep down wanted it.

A female offender tells herself that girls can't hurt guys and that because her victim ejaculated, he had a good time. A male offender tells himself all girls play hard to get and that she needed to get laid anyway. All of these myths and lies did not formulate in a vacuum, they are the messages we hear from friends, the media, and even our legal system.

Christopher McFadden was a judge in a rape and sodomy case in 2011. After reviewing the files he stated that the victim's behavior wasn't how he "thinks a rape victim should act." The victim had Down syndrome.

In 2018 State Superior Court Judge John Russo asked a rape victim, "Do you know how to stop somebody from having intercourse with you? Close your legs? Call the police? Did you do any of those things?"

In 2019, in Kansas, Leavenworth County District Judge Michael Gibbens said, "I do find that the victims in this case are more of an aggressor than a participant in the criminal conduct." The case was for thirteen and fourteen-year-old girls who were raped by a sixty-seven-year-old man.

Toxic beliefs about gender are rampant in our culture; they permeate every corner of our lives and our world. Whenever we are faced with concerns that are touted as "human nature" or "the way things have always been" we should put on our sociology/anthropology hat and go digging for answers to these assumptions. Are all cultures/communities victims to toxic gender expectations and roles?

The answer is no. While no culture is perfect, we can certainly glean numerous insights into how we, as Western colonialized society, can grow and evolve in what we think is inherently male or female.

As mentioned in chapter 1, there are important insights into how toxic gender roles can sway us to either be rape cultures or rape-free cultures. But separate from sexual violence there are many examples of societies where women are seen in a more masculine light and men take on what we would consider feminine roles without being seen as lesser or emasculated.

Take, for example, the Aka Pygmy Tribe in the Republic of Congo. The women in the tribe are known for the tracking and hunting abilities, often achieving status as hunters that outshine those of the men. The men of the Aka Tribe share equally with their partners in all aspects of family life including some of the most intimate and gendered parts of child-rearing. In the Western world we often talk about how a father who changes a diaper or talks to his children about their feelings is the gold standard for an evolved and involved dad.

The Aka pygmies do all of these things including breastfeeding.[9] Yes, you read that right, the father's offer their breast to their children. While they do not produce much milk, as male milk ducts are much smaller and not stimulated by birth hormones, they offer their nipple to their babies none the less knowing it will provide comfort and connection and occasionally some sustenance.

The goal here is not to force all fathers to get comfortable with an infant suckling their breast, though it couldn't hurt. It is to reimagine how we think of gender, what we consider "normal," and natural, as well as the ways that we consider the kind of culture and world we want to create. One in which gender is not used to constrict or force conformity but wherever person is given an inalienable right to express and explore the entire gamut of the human experience.

GENDER IN THE BEDROOM

One of the more detrimental ways that toxic expressions of gender play out is in our beliefs and scripts around sex and dating. Sexual scripting is a fancy social science term that explains how we follow certain consistent ways of interacting and communicating on specific topics with specific people. For example, you follow a script when you meet someone, when you answer the phone, and how you ask someone on a date.

Much of our response is influenced by our identity and the identities of those around us. How we expect to interact with our kids versus our boss on Monday morning follows a very different script.

The same is true for whether we identify as men or women, masculine or feminine, and gay or straight, and so on. Each role gives us a different acceptable script. For example, a man walking up to a woman at a party and asking her a question to spark a conversation is seen as natural. A woman doing the same to a man is seen as bold if not desperate.

A woman telling a male partner she doesn't want to have sex yet or tonight is seen as common and acceptable. A man doing the same is asked if he is gay, and what is wrong with him? Does he not like her or does he not like women? Deviate from the script and you face consequences. Society, all societies, have different gender scripting but are all very good at teaching us from a very young age what those scripts are and why we must not deviate from them.

As humans, we have evolved to seek acceptance from our tribe. In a prehistoric world it meant life or death and even in a postindustrial age we know we must find a community or likely perish. This need to be included and accepted drives the way we date and mate, and if our scripts themselves become toxic, so too will our ways of communicating and respecting each other.

THE EFFECTS OF TOKENISM

Consent has for a long time been ignored, mocked, or erased from our sexual scripting. This is true for all gender identities. One of the ways that we see consent being invalidated in our sexual scripting is explained in the concepts called "token resistance" and "token compliance." Tokenism is the idea of doing something just because you have been told you should, not because you mean it.

For example, if you are bringing a woman into a board meeting just to have a woman there because only men had been invited. That is tokenizing the one woman who is present instead of bringing in qualified people from diverse gender and social backgrounds to have a myriad of perspectives. Tokenism in sexual scripting means to give the response you think you have to say in order to maintain social acceptability.

For woman/girls, this means to be pleasing but not aggressive or overtly sexual. Women are told they should put up some resistance, say no at first, try to make their partner wait but just not too long. A woman who asks for sex too soon has sex too much or demands sexual pleasure is vilified. The female partner's sexual script requires a false "no"; no to needing sex, no to multiple partners, no to prioritizing sex that satisfies her body. This leads to the connection between a woman saying "no" and her not really meaning it. While that is a hugely problematic statement rooted in rape ideology, it also points out how sexual scripting has toxic elements which do not allow women to communicate a valid "no" or "yes" without consequences.

For men/boys, their sexual script is flipped. Men are socialized to say yes—yes to all sex at all times. Even if it isn't in a form that they want or with someone they want to be with, even if they are being exploited, they are drawn as sexually insatiable and thus always grateful for what they can get.

Men/boys are expected to always be ready to penetrate their partner, be grateful for whatever sex they can get, and never want to be on the submissive or receiving end. Because the penis becomes visibly aroused and ejaculation happens from most sexual stimulation men are told that their neurological reactions are akin to affirmative consent.

Men are ostracized and humiliated for not wanting sex, wanting to be penetrated, or for being sexually stimulated against their will. This means that men have many interactions that are sexually abusive or assaultive but rarely describe them that way. That they had to go along with it they tell themselves, they had an orgasm so it must have been what they wanted, and their true needs or desires should never be revealed. For men saying "yes" is often forced, tokenized, and weaponized.

To change these, we must first acknowledge the problem and decide how to create pathways for improving authentic communication between all parties. Even in relationships where there are two men or two women the toxic scripting from heterosexual dynamics still plays out. Lesbians both feel pressured to come off as not too sexual; gay men can find asking to wait on sex as taboo in the community. Even when we think we have escaped a script the internalization of those messages persists.

NONBINARY EXPERIENCES

Let us examine the other side of what we just discussed; because of full disclosure, everything you just read was built on another social misunderstanding, the construct of gender being binary. The idea that gender fits neatly into two boxes and that sex and gender are always congruent is a pretty recent fad. It is not how the majority of societies have seen things for most of human history. When colonization went global in the fourteenth to seventeenth centuries gender and sex became controlled by European Christians.

Colonizers got in their boats and sailed the globe spreading disease, gender binaries, and the patriarchy. Before colonization, many indigenous societies accepted, and celebrated, that there were three to five genders. All across the globe, human societies knew full and well that people are far too complicated and nuanced to have only two options for anything, it was normal to watch a child grow up and be feminine in a male body or masculine in a female body. Whatever role that person then decided to take on in their tribe was seen as their choice.

Many indigenous tribes in North America called people outside of male or female boxes as two-spirited (a term still used today). Two-spirited people were not merely accepted or tolerated; they were seen as spiritual leaders and visionaries. The term comes from the concept that people who exist outside of being strictly male or female have not one soul but two.

This gives them a unique ability to see the world from both a male and female lens and gives them a deeper relationship to God. Tribal leaders ask two-spirited members to provide them with guidance on community issues and help with the spiritual wellness of the tribe. Two-spirited people are most often compared to transgender people today but can also include lesbian, gay, and bisexual individuals as they often express their gender, even solely in the fact of loving someone of the same sex, in a nonconforming way. Understanding this history is important when it comes to consent, because so often what we believe is typically male or female is just society's modern expectations.

Separate from historical context is the hard science that chromosomes do not believe in a gender binary either. Chromosomes do not stick to the XX or XY boxes in millions of people. When chromosomes go outside the binary, it is called intersexuality. Intersex people have bodies, and often genitals or reproductive organs, that are a unique blend of what we commonly think of as male or female.

This means that they are literally, on a medical level, neither male nor female. This is not expression or preference—these are the cold hard facts. For years, who were neither male nor female at birth were called hermaphrodites. This was a derogatory term from day one and is not used anymore.

Doctors told parents they could guess or "test" their babies and tell them if they had a boy or girl. They would then mutilate their perfect bodies to fit what society deems as acceptable genitalia. Ambiguous genitalia is not unhealthy, unnatural, or in need or correcting. Corrective surgeries can cause intense trauma and leave lifelong nerve damage.

Today, intersex activists are changing this narrative. They are speaking to parents and surgeons on behalf of their children and younger selves and demanding that they let their babies grow up the way they were made, loving their bodies for their uniqueness instead of seeing how they need to confirm. In this, they also help us deconstruct gender—from the ground up.

For those who transition across the binary—going from male to female or female to male within their lifetime—the experience of navigating sex, scripting, and consent from the vantage point of both gender extremes are enlightening. For those who do not prescribe to any one gender, this takes on another dimension.

When it comes to victimization no one in America (or in almost anywhere on earth) is more likely to be abused, raped, or murdered than transgender women. This says so much about how gender plays into violence, consent, and the value of a person's life based on their identity and expression. Trans women have made three significant transgressions in society's eyes—first, they chose to leave the best gender to go to the worst (male to female), second, they refuse to stick to the script of sex and gender being the same, and third, they make heterosexuality something that can't be defined by attraction to sex only. We value maleness and masculinity so much—that is why we elect, promote, hire, and glorify men to such a higher degree.

To make a decision to openly identify as female and stop claiming your given male identity means going from the best to the worst by society's standards, and that has everything to do with why cisgender women, feminine men, and trans women are the most likely to be abused and assaulted; their worth is so minuscule. To transition from your assigned gender to your true identity flies in the face of everything we were taught as little children about gender.

Add to this that now men who identify as heterosexual might be attracted to the gender expression of this person only to discover that their sex and gender are not the same and you have a recipe for an eruption of the ultimate evil of TM—murder. Men, feeling that this complicates their privilege as a straight male, act out in rage.

They say they were tricked but what they mean is they can't accept that their sexual desires are outside of what they may have previously thought. There is no documented risk with a trans male coming out to a female partner. She might be upset, but there is no national homicide statistic on this. Why? Because women are permitted to have fluidity within their sexuality and do not have the same kind of threat to their identity by acknowledging a range of attraction to different identities or expressions

DISCUSSING GENDER IS VITAL TO CONSENT

We've begun to raise daughters more like sons . . . but few have the courage to raise our sons more like our daughters.

—Gloria Steinem

Gender is a significant factor when it comes to bringing consent conversations to the next level and working to actually heal not just patch up the wound, that is, sexual misconduct and rape culture. We gender children from birth. Our homes, classrooms, and communities continue to send toxic gender messages to both our children but also to us. The first step in addressing this begins within.

We must work to examine our personal gender biases, expectations, and scripts before we can teach the next generation how to do things right. We may ourselves still snicker at a joke about male sexual assault because we rarely recognize it as anything worse than a punch line. Many of us still think of "real sex" as a woman receiving a male partner and genital penetration and feel grossed out by consensual sexual behavior that goes outside of this script. If we still ask "do you think that's a man or a woman" instead of not giving a damn we still have a lot of work to do.

Here is the great news about starting with your own unlearning—it allows you to model this to your children and students. They can observe you working through your biases. Tell them when you made an assumption when you have a realization that you still have concerns about how you are perceived, and where you notice this in society (especially in the media). Tell them when it is hard and explain why it is essential to growth. Let your children have conversations with you about both of your following questions:

1. Should men pay for every date with a woman? Every first date? Things to consider include gender pay gaps, who initiates and who accepts the date, and options for healthy gender role expression. Discuss if both parties are male or female, then what?

2. What is the purpose of gendering bathrooms? How does this impact trans, intersex, and gender nonconforming people who face high rates of violence? What could a safe and private space for people of every gender look like? Could this help parents with kids of different genders who don't want them to go into a bathroom alone?

3. How do you define your gender? What does being male or female mean to you? Where has it enhanced your life and where has it held you back? Should we have separate standards for being a good man or woman or should there be a "good human" standard?

4. What do cartoons, movies, music tell us about how boys/girls and men/woman should behave? What stereotypes do we see being promoted? What if the men and women switched roles/lines? How would that make us feel?

5. What does society tell us about how men/women differ in sexual desire, libido, and pleasure? How easy is it to ask for or give honest and affirmative consent? Why is it hard?

There are no right or wrong answers to these questions. Remember this is a discussion, allow your children to disagree with you and have their own conclusions. Ask them again in a few years and see how the conversation has evolved.

Gender is not the enemy—bias, stereotypes, hierarchies, and oppression are. We are not asking for gender to not exist; we are asking for it to be limitless instead of limiting. In creating a vast and expansive terrain for gender to unfold in we take away the aspects that can make it a toxic social construct.

In a world where gender is expansive, instead of restrictive, we see a sharp decline in interpersonal violence. We observe relationships— from families to colleagues to spouses—that are mutually respectful and beneficial. No one feels drained, threatened, or manipulated by connecting to another. If these standards become the norm then behaviors such as sexual violence and domestic violence are extinguished.

Human beings are conditioned to seek out what is considered socially acceptable, the reason being that we need each other. If dominance and control over others is what gives us social power, we will follow along. If fearful submission makes us acceptable to our community, we will follow along. If kindness, empowerment, and reverence for one another is the norm, we will follow that too. The choice is ours.

TAKEAWAYS FROM CHAPTER 6

- Gender roles, for better or worse, are all around us.
- Beliefs about sex and gender impact us from in utero.
- Gender expression and expectations impact every part of our life: from how easily we can access a bathroom to how we can communicate our needs in intimate relationships.
- Most people grew up with a limited view on gender believing it to be binary.
- Medicine, psychology, history, and anthropology all can inform us that gender is not binary but far more complex and expansive.

- By deconstructing and unlearning our own toxic beliefs about gender we can redefine what gender means in a healthy and holistic way.
- Gender itself is not toxic, beliefs about gender that force people to not be empathic, expressive, or have full personal agency are.

NOTES

1. Richardson, S. S. (2012). Sexing the X: How the X became the "female chromosome." *Signs: Journal of Women in Culture and Society, 37*(4), 909–933.

2. Steele, C. M., & Aronson, J. (1995). Stereotype threat and the intellectual test performance of African Americans. *Journal of Personality and Social Psychology, 69*(5), 797.
The Glass Hammer. Why Stereotype Threat Keeps Girls Out of Math and Science, and What to Do About It. *By Melissa J. Anderson*

3. Werner, A., & Malterud, K. (2003). It is hard work behaving as a credible patient: Encounters between women with chronic pain and their doctors. *Social Science & Medicine, 57*(8), 1409–1419.

4. Hochschild, A., & Machung, A. (2012). *The Second Shift: Working Families and the Revolution At Home*. Penguin.

5. Craig, L. (2007). Is there really a second shift, and if so, who does it? A time-diary investigation. *Feminist Review, 86*(1), 149–170.

6. Kupers, T. A. (2005). Toxic masculinity as a barrier to mental health treatment in prison. *Journal of Clinical Psychology, 61*(6), 713–724.

7. Parent, M. C., Gobble, T. D., & Rochlen, A. (2019). Social media behavior, toxic masculinity, and depression. *Psychology of Men & Masculinities, 20*(3), 277.

8. Good, C., Aronson, J., & Inzlicht, M. (2003). Improving adolescents' standardized test performance: An intervention to reduce the effects of stereotype threat. *Journal of Applied Developmental Psychology, 24*(6), 645–662.
Taillandier-Schmitt, A., Esnard, C., & Mokounkolo, R. (2012). Self-affirmation in occupational training: Effects on the math performance of French women nurses under stereotype threat. *Sex Roles, 67*(1–2), 43–57.

9. Hewlett, B. S. (1993). *Intimate Fathers: The Nature and Context of Aka Pygmy Paternal Infant Care*. Ann Arbor, MI: University of Michigan Press.

Chapter 7

The Future We Create

We made it. Seven chapters of discussion and discourse on teaching affirmative consent to children and teens. Whether you are a parent, teacher, or administrator you are hopefully feeling excited and ready to engage in this vital work. The tools in this book are designed to give you a launching point, a place to get started from. What that means is that there will be more work to be done after this.

Consent education is vast, complex, and emotionally exhausting. Take it from someone who has dedicated their entire professional career to this topic. You will need to rest and pace yourself, so you don't burn out. It is easy to feel on fire after reading a book like this or attending a seminar or conference on the subject. You feel ready and charged up, you want to go full force ahead, but once you face the sea of obstacles, red tape, and opposition you may feel all of that joy being replaced by frustration and even bitterness.

In the play *A Memory, A Monologue, A Rant, A Prayer* by Eve Ensler, The First Kiss monologue is about a six-year-old girl who is sexually abused by her camp counselor. The little girl is forcibly French-kissed by the counselor in front of her peers. The trauma of this causes her to urinate on herself, for which she is further humiliated and abused by the staff member.

May my daughters first kiss
May your daughter's first kiss
May everyone's daughter's first kiss
Be anticipated and wanted[1]

Such a simple wish, and yet still heartbreakingly elusive. In 2019 a study that looked at whether a first sexual experience was forced/coerced or voluntary found that of over thirteen thousand participants one in sixteen were sexually assaulted the first time they had sex.[2] The study found that compared to women with voluntary sexual initiation, women with forced sexual initiation were more likely to experience an unwanted first pregnancy, abortion, endometriosis, pelvic inflammatory disease, problems with ovulation or menstruation, illicit drug use, fair or poor health, and difficulty completing tasks. Even one sexually traumatic experience can alter someone's life indefinitely.

This is why we must take up the arms of education and empowerment to not accept the reasoning or excuses for putting off or ignoring consent education in our homes, communities, and schools. Whether our babies are six, sixteen, or sixty sexual abuse and coercion are life-long problems that will not go away on their own. Education is not a cure-all—the systems that we report to must be on the same page as educators and victims.

Communities must support survivors and hold abuser accountable. Consequences for abuse must seek to heal all parties involved, seeking restoration in justice not just empty punitive actions.

You may be surprised from where you face opposition. The allies you thought you had in your pocket may suddenly back out. The people who preach consent culture values may not want to partner with you unless they are the star of the show. If you are seen as a more credentialed expert than them, they may get jealous and try to sabotage your efforts. We say this from years of experience, every one of those examples has happened to us more than once.

There are days and months where it is human to sincerely wonder if we should do something else for a career. In the early days of our work, we especially might think we will do sexual violence prevention work for a few years and then switch to something easier to digest.

You might be a parent who wants to get into advocacy, a principal looking to explore educational reform, or a teacher passionate about infusing these topics into your state curriculum. Whoever you are and wherever you have been planted know that what you are called to do is needed. Many admire this work, but only a tiny percentage wants to dedicate their lives to it. We need you.

COMMUNITY ACTIVISM: FROM BOOK CLUBS TO STUDENT ORGANIZATIONS

The question you are facing now is where to go first or next. In this chapter, we will explore the different avenues for beginning and enhancing this work no matter what your platform is. Some you may have already been trying and others you may just be getting started with while a few of you may have never imagined or dreamed of. We hope that this gives you an actionable outline that you can use to get started. If you get stuck or need further support, please reach out through the contact information in the about the author section in the back of this book.

When people think of community advocacy, they often imagine meetings late in the evening painting posters, marches in the streets, and soapboxes and megaphones. Community activism can and does sometimes involve those things, but it is so much more than that.

To create a culture of consent, you will need to get multiple dimensions of stakeholders involved. Students, staff, faculty, parents, religious congregations, and grassroots groups are a few to start with. It is easy to look at that list and think that they are all way too different and will never sit in a room together, well not peacefully at least.

If that is your line of thinking you can give up now because to create the change you have to be able to find common ground among many different people and groups. Yes, this means there may be heated discussions and that some will drop out because they won't compromise, but that is the natural evolution of a movement.

Come to the table with as many facts as you can, stay away from strictly trying to pull at their heartstrings—everyone heart plays in a different key. Armed with your facts and clear plan make sure that you do not carry combative energy. Make this an approachable discussion and be patient answering questions you may find shockingly ignorant or offensive. Trust me, we hear them all the time, and while we may never get over how many bizarre beliefs people still hold dear, we can now roll with the tide and address them calmly.

Even though this book is written with teachers and parents in mind, we hope that maybe a few students have picked it up too. High school is such a great time to start your work in community activism. When that fire is ignited in you when you are young, you have fuel to burn. Do not feel like you are too young or uninformed to advocate for consent education in your area; in fact, go bigger; try speaking at your city council meeting or state legislature. Student voices speak volumes.

Maeve Sanford-Kelly was a twelve-year-old middle school student when she realized the impact of rape culture on the world she was growing up in. She witnessed cases such as the miscarriage of justice that was the Brock Turner trial and how predators like Bill Cosby were allowed to create systems that allowed them to not only operate but flourish in their violent deeds. Maeve was "just a kid" but refused to let these observations go.

In 2018, at the age of fourteen, Maeve testified in front of the Montgomery County Delegation for a bill that would require consent education for all seventh- and tenth-grade students. Maeve stated, "Before we are taught about pregnancy prevention and STDs, we have to be taught about consent." The bill died on a state level, with Republican and conservative democrats causing its demise, but two school districts in the state voluntarily adopted it. Success is not easily fought for, there will be setbacks, but student voices are powerful and can change the world.

No matter your title or role here are some ideas for getting a consent culture movement started in your area:

Parent Teacher Associations (PTAs)

Parent Teacher Associations (PTAs) are powerful and important avenues for bringing forth systemic change in educational environments. Many people, being long disillusioned with PTAs, will roll their eyes at the idea of anything beyond performative measures coming from these kinds of meetings. Despite this jaded outlook we must still firmly believe in the power of parent/teacher collaboration and allyship.

Parents and teacher have the most important thing in their life in common—the youth that they are entrusted to protect, guide, and educate. Many teachers fear that bringing consent education into a school environment will anger parents, but research tells us that even within the framework of sexuality education, most parents want their children to be informed and responsible members of society.

In 2019 The Alabama Campaign to Prevent Teen Pregnancy worked with the University of South Alabama to survey parents in one of the most conservative states in the deep south on what they want included in their children's sex education.[3] Alabama remains a strictly abstinence-only education state, no discussion of contraception, pregnancy, STDs, sexual orientation, much less consent and sexual violence can be discussed in public schools.

Parents in the state were surveyed and their desires for what they want their children to learn very much contradicted the state standards. Over 98 percent of parents survey felt that sex education was important or very important, 99 percent wanted birth control and STDs to be discussed, 98 percent agreed with talking about rape and sexual assault, and 90 percent said it was important to talk about sexual orientations—not exactly abstinence-only education promoting.

By blending PTA organizations with the following complementary grassroots tools parents, teachers, and students will often find they share more common cares and concerns than they previously imagined.

Councils

Councils are a big thing in the advocacy world. They allow multiple individuals and agencies invested in similar work and aligned objectives to meet, talk, and collaborate.

One of the common misconceptions with councils is that you have to be an executive director or professor to start or chair (lead) one. You don't! Anyone who is good at organizing a group and showing up consistently with a list of things to talk about can form a council or committee. You need to start by scouting a location and setting a time you can regularly meet. Inconsistent meeting times will cause people to stop showing up.

Identify people you want to attend—don't be afraid to reach out to those influential executive directors and academics. Even if they can't attend, they will send someone from their organization. Make the meeting organized and with focused discussion points. Lastly, invite speakers or do excursions into the community to make it all the more worth the while for your members.

Book Clubs

A book club or learning circle is a great way to get started if you are working with a community that has no foundational understanding about these topics. Don't have any experts or activists? Make some! Find a reading list of books that cover different aspects of this topic and read them together. This is a super interesting and engaging way for people to be introduced to a sensitive conversation.

It is also easier to have debates or discussions in an environment like this versus in front of a speaker. In a book club, there will be a leader, but everyone's voice is on an equal playing field. Giving people time to digest this information through reading privately will also help cut down on defensive or caustic attitudes. Just don't forget to include this book in your list (wink, wink).

Student Organizations

Now for our dear students, we have not forgotten about you. Do you know that many of the social movements you are experiencing today came from your parents' and grandparents' generations in their high school and college years? Nothing is new under the sun, but time causes us old folks to forget how we once had such optimism for the transformations we wanted to see in the world. Remind us! Student organizations are an incredible way to create change.

Ask your school if you can start a club there, if not do not despair, start one at your local library or meet in a coffee shop. The same guidelines that apply to the councils apply here, just because you are young does not mean you care any less if something is well put together or not. If at all possible ask a seasoned activist/organizer to help you get started. They can show you how to lead a meeting, create an agenda, and outline your purpose and mission. If there is no one in your area e-mail people (you can e-mail me). Ask for their advice and maybe even raise some money to have them come visit and present for you.

Yes, it can be hard to be young because people expect so little from you, but then combat that and blow their minds. One day you may be hosting a conference for consent in your city!

CURRICULUM ADVOCACY

Advocating to improve your current curricula may seem like something that is out of your reach. It is usually the county and state Department of Education that gets to decide what is and is not included. If you are at a private school or a charter school, you will have more freedom in choosing what is included in your school's curriculum, but you still have to get board members parents and your community on board. Remember to refer to the previous steps without creating community and stakeholder buy-in.

Start small, remember even one option for us gives people the ability to put the toe in the water and have a taste of what their potential could be. This is great for getting people to come over to your side especially when you are in an area that has a lot of hesitation or concerns around consent as a topic.

One of the main concerns will be this part of sex education. As mentioned before consent education should be included in sexual conversations and a health curriculum but if that is not a natural bridge for you to cross you can make consent course utterly separate from sexuality. We have had school administrators tell us that they cannot expand their sex education because their county does not support it but that if consent is taught through a safety and awareness lens, then more parents will be open to it. Remember to make this distinction—that consent does not have to be sex education.

Even though you are starting small, this is another opportunity to plant an important seed that can grow into something much bigger. When you begin your consent education course make sure that it is being assessed. One of the most common mistakes people make when they start initiatives and organizing is that they don't do any research into what they are doing. If you want money or political backing for your efforts, you have to show people the numbers, pulling at the heartstrings and trying to explain why, theoretically, you think this is a great idea is not going to impact them the same way statistics will.

This does not mean you have to hire a fancy assessment firm to do a longitudinal study on your course. It can be as simple as doing a pre- and post-survey showing the change in the students' understanding of consent as a topic. If you have people who are willing to volunteer some time and have experience with the research, you can also do some focus groups.

Ask the students in the course upfront what they think consent is, what they want to learn on, what concerns they have, and then bring the same focus group together in the middle of the course, ask the same questions, note the difference in response, and do a final evaluation after the course is completed. If you can try, go even a few months later or a year later and see how the information was retained.

It is also great to know how it was applied, are the students using this in their real-life interactions, if not what are the barriers to that, and how could the course be improved. You want to take notes making sure that you have permission from the guardians of each of the students up front. And then you will need help with what is called coding and finding themes in the recorded responses. This together with your quantitative, or numbers-based, research from the surveys will provide a mixed method scholarly and well-founded foundation for your argument to progress this curriculum further.

Once you have the staff on your side, you can also use it to approach your state representatives and officials to bring this to a broader audience. While writing this book, we are waiting on an appropriations bill that aims to bring consent education to our k-12 schools.

You do not need a lot of connections to do this; you have to knock in enough doors and bring the research you have gathered to build your argument for it. Representatives have to bring forth and sponsor a certain number of bills each term and appropriations per request (APR) can allow you the financial backing from your state to move forward with projects that you are passionate about and you see a need for in your community.

STARTING IN THE HOME AND CLASSROOM

If you want to change the world, go home and love your family.

—Mother Teresa

It is easy to get excited about global ideas, that is, the macro. The dreams of changing state and federal policy: writing life-changing curriculum, watching rates of trafficking and assault drastically drop in your city, and being asked to do a TED talk on how you read this book and went out and transformed your world.

Change doesn't usually work that way though; change requires the micro. Explosive movements—that get quick and powerful press coverage—often soon burn out. Attention is paid so intensely and so quickly that it cannot last, the media is bombarded, activists are fatigued, and society senses oversaturation.

It isn't glamorous, and it isn't often exciting, but bring changes in your home and your classroom. Yes, not even your neighborhood, your grade, or your school. Change has to grow its roots in the soil of your family and class before it can blossom and bloom in the world around you. Start now, put this book down and have a conversation with your family about consent.

Look at your lesson plan and find a way to infuse the topic of interpersonal communication; if you can't do that bring up current events with your class or listen to their conversations and clarify and redirect when you hear them make comments that are founded in a rape-myth acceptance paradigm. Rest assured there are opportunities every week, if not every day for you to build these bridges and make these conversations normal.

A bit of a warning though—be prepared to face the floodgates. Once you start talking about consent, bodily autonomy, and preventing sexual and domestic abuse people of all ages will begin pouring out of the woodwork to tell you about what happened to them. People are hungry for spaces that they can share their story safely in.

When #MeToo hit social media like a wave in 2017 many people responded that they couldn't believe these many women that they knew were survivors. The vast numbers of victims that the movement was highlighting didn't add up to them, nor how they could only be hearing about the depth and breadth of this problem now. In all honesty, though, we are often not surprised that people don't see what we see. Survivors are watching and listening to everyone all around them at all times.

They see your comment on a story about survivors where you blamed the victim, they notice who doesn't post in support of sexual assault awareness month, and they can tell who is likely to believe and support them and who is not. The people who spread seeds of doubt are also the people no one discloses to, those who do continuously verbalize their support will know how the statistics are a small slice of how significant this problem really is.

We have so little control over the systems and powers that be. Fighting the good fight means years and years of effort and energy, often to zero net gain. What we can control much more efficiently is the micro: the microcosmic world that we are in charge of. We cannot silence the naysayers or critics forever.

Even when we win battles, there is always a new opponent on the horizon. In our homes, in our classrooms, we master universes. We can plant seeds over and over knowing that the winds of the outside world will blow 80 percent of them away. Still, the 20 percent of the message we teach the children in our lives does stick, and that can mean the literal difference between someone continuing to perpetuate rape culture and the next generation building the framework for a culture of consent.

TAKEAWAYS FROM CHAPTER 7

- Consent education is vast, complex, and emotionally exhausting.
- Opposition can come from many places. By preparing yourself for this reality you can overcome the obstacles before you.
- Self-care is vital. You need to have a plan in place for what is ahead, or you will burnout and your efforts will be for naught.
- Community advocacy is the foundation for systemic change.
- There are many ways to bringing your community onboard—from councils to book clubs.
- Education and opportunities for dialogue are the cornerstones for buy-in.
- If you are in a school setting, advocating for consent to be infused into the curriculum is key to changing cultural norms and scripts.
- Students often underestimate how much clout and influence they have.
- Student organizations can often advocate for changes that teachers and administrators are hesitant to ask.
- Ultimately all change starts within.
- We must first relearn our own understanding of consent, boundaries, and personal autonomy.
- By starting in the micro—with our homes and classrooms—we can have a profound and lasting impact that ripples into the larger spheres of influence.
- This work is not easy, but it is always worth it.

NOTES

1. Ensler, E. (Ed.). (2008). *A Memory, a Monologue, a Rant, and a Prayer: Writings to Stop Violence Against Women and Girls.* Villard.

2. Hawks, L., Woolhandler, S., Himmelstein, D. U., Bor, D. H., Gaffney, A., & McCormick, D. Association between forced sexual initiation and health outcomes among US women. *JAMA Intern Med.* Published online September 16, 2019. doi:10.1001/jamainternmed.2019.3500.

3. http://alabamacampaign.org/wp-content/uploads/2017/08/Alabama-Parental-Attitudes-Study.pdf.

About the Author

Dr. Laura McGuire is a nationally recognized sexuality educator, trauma-informed specialist, and inclusion consultant. She has worked as an instructor, presenter, educator, consultant, and trainer.

In 2011 she earned her GED and in less than five years later she earned her doctorate in education. Dr. McGuire earned her bachelor's degree in social sciences from Thomas Edison State University and her graduate degrees in educational leadership for change from Fielding Graduate University. Her doctoral dissertation, entitled "Seen but Not Heard: Pathways to Improve Inclusion of LGBT Persons and Sexual Trauma Survivors in Sexual Health Education," examined the marginalization of sexual minorities within health education on a global scale.

Dr. McGuire is a certified full-spectrum doula, professional teacher, certified sexual health educator, and vinyasa yoga instructor. Her experiences include both public and private sectors, middle schools, high schools, and university settings. In 2015, she served as the first sexual violence prevention and education program manager at the University of Houston, and in 2017, she became the first victim advocate/prevention educator at the U.S. Merchant Marine Academy.

She is a member of the American Association of Sexuality Educators, Counselors and Therapists (AASECT); chair of the AASECT Diversity, Equity, and Inclusion Committee; and a member of the

Society of Professional Consultants. Dr. McGuire lives in the United States, with her two children and two dogs, where she works as a full-time consultant, author, professor, and expert witness at the National Center for Equity and Agency.

She can be contacted at info@drlauramcguire.com